COOKING OF PROVENCE

PATRICIA
LOUSADA

CONTENTS

Published exclusively for J Sainsbury plc
Stamford House Stamford Street
London SE1 9LL
by Martin Books
Simon & Schuster Consumer Group
Grafton House 64 Maids Causeway
Cambridge CB5 8DD

First published 1993

ISBN 0 85941 804 9

Printed in Italy by Printer Trento

THE AUTHOR

Photo: Eileen Tweedy

Lady Lousada was born in New York City. Her Italian mother was a singer and an inspired cook with a wide knowledge of Italian and French cuisine. Patricia was a member of the New York City Ballet and her fellow dancers' love of good food further involved her in cooking. She later lived in Paris for two years, where the experience of attending lectures at the Cordon Bleu school, against a background of Parisian restaurants, deepened her interest still more. She has given lectures and demonstrations on various kinds of cooking.

Patricia has written a number of cookery books, the latest being *The Dinner Party Book*. *The Cooking of Provence* is the sixth book she has written exclusively for Sainsbury's; her earlier titles include *Pasta Italian-Style* and *The Chocolate Lover's Cookbook*. Lady Lousada lives in London with her English husband and has four children.

Pictured on the front cover: clockwise from top left, Pistou (Basil, garlic and parmesan sauce, page 19), Aïoli (Garlic mayonnaise, page 18), Anchoïade (Anchovy spread, page 20) and Tapenade (Olive and anchovy spread, page 20).

Pictured on the back cover: Tarte aux Poires Renversée (Caramelised upside-down pear tart, page 84), Tarte aux Fruits (Fruit tart, page 83).

Note on recipes
All recipes in this book give ingredients in both metric (g, ml, etc.) and imperial (oz, pints, etc.) measures. Use either set of quantities, but not both, in any one recipe.

All teaspoons and tablespoons are level, unless otherwise stated. 1 teaspoon = a 5 ml spoon; 1 tablespoon = a 15 ml spoon.

Egg size is medium (size 3), unless otherwise stated.

Vegetables are medium size, unless otherwise stated.

Freshly ground black pepper should be used for pepper throughout.

Great care should be taken when preparing chillies. Wear rubber gloves if necessary, and wash hands thoroughly afterwards. Be careful not to touch your eyes.

INTRODUCTION

My first experience of France, indeed of Europe, was a summer spent near Nice when I was in my late twenties. It was in every way a time of discovery. I was dazzled by everything – the light, the vegetation, the incredibly blue water, the pastel-coloured houses with their green and blue shutters, and most of all by the food. I had never tasted anything like the fragrant onion tarts, the fish stews, the orange-flavoured daubes, the stuffed courgette flowers or the fresh figs. I had never before seen a lemon tree growing, or a sea-urchin served in its spiny half-shell. Nor had I experienced a wind like the Mistral, which causes cream to turn and moods to blacken. It is said to blow for three days out of every ten, but I was lucky and only experienced a few days of it. I explored a few parts of Provence that summer but it was only on later visits that I became aware of the range of Provence's natural beauty and the extent of its cuisine.

Provence is bordered on three sides by natural boundaries: the Alps to the east, the Mediterranean to the south, and the Rhône valley to the west, from Montélimar down to Marseilles. Within this area distinct regions co-exist, each with its own peculiar character. Along the Rhône valley grape vines and olive trees flourish, and everywhere the air is heavy with the scent of flowered herbs growing wild over the hills. When one walks across even the most arid land the fragrance from the herbs crushed underfoot rises up, balmy and delicious. These are Cézanne's great hills, stark and enigmatic. In the fertile plains around Avignon abundant fruit and vegetables are grown, while in the north there is pasture land, fields of wheat and even truffles under dwarf oak trees. And everywhere are clumps of lavender sounding with the hum of honey bees.

Provençal cuisine draws its strength from using the freshest natural ingredients. In

Preparation and cooking times

Preparation and cooking times are included at the heads of the recipes as a general guide; preparation times, especially, are approximate and timings are usually rounded to the nearest 5 minutes.

Preparation times include the time taken to prepare ingredients in the list, but not to make any 'basic' recipe, such as stock.

The cooking times given at the heads of the recipes denote cooking periods when the dish can be left largely unattended, e.g. baking, stewing, and not the total amount of cooking for the recipe. Always read and follow the timings given for the steps of the recipe in the method.

addition to local speciality shops and bakeries, each town has its daily or weekly market for fresh produce. They are wonderful to visit: everyone is there, and the town's squares come alive with the cries of vendors selling all sorts of different and enticing foods. There are olives of all sizes, shining black in vats of oil, or green ones crushed with fennel seeds, and little goat's cheeses flavoured with garlic or rolled in herbs. There are vegetables in vivid colours: yellow and red peppers, fine green beans, mauve-green artichokes and wild mushrooms, as well as the dark leafy *blettes* or swiss chard, which features in so many of the local dishes. On another stall a woman sells little bunches of assorted wild leaves, such as young lettuce, dandelion and rocket, for making *mesclun* salad. There are pyramids of lemons, and baskets of figs, plums and melons. There are stalls selling slabs of hot, freshly baked socca, a golden chick-pea flour pancake found only in Provence. And of course there are fish – everything from salted anchovies and inexpensive sardines to fresh and glistening Mediterranean-caught specialities like *poissons de roches* used in the making of local bouillabaisse.

It has been a long time since Greek settlers founded the port of Marseilles and ancient Romans named the region *Provincia Romana*, but foreign influences have left their mark on the cooking style of Provence as much as the intensity of the Mediterranean sun has. Provençal ravioli have kept their name as well as their shape, but are stuffed with swiss chard leaves or orange-flavoured beef; pistou is a close relation of the Genovese pesto sauce, and even couscous from North Africa has for generations been incorporated into the local repertoire .

With the brilliant array of vegetable and fruit available here in our own markets and supermarkets, it is possible to create authentic-tasting Provençal dishes. It is a healthy cuisine which contains very little butter or cream and a good deal of health-giving olive oil. It is also a simple cuisine – many Provençal dishes can be prepared quickly and yet are tasty and attractive. It has given me great pleasure to cook and eat the dishes in this book and I hope they will provide the same enjoyment for you and your family and friends.

INGREDIENTS

OLIVE OIL
Using the traditional method, the olives (about 100 lb from each mature tree) are ground to a paste between granite millstones. The extracted oil is then separated from its watery juices in a centrifuge. The oil produced in this 'first cold pressing' is the finest of all. Hot water is poured on the paste that remains after the first pressing, and spun again to produce the 'second pressing'. The stone mill method is now only used by some single-estate producers or small village co-operatives. This oil is the highest quality, but it is produced in small quantities, is harder to find and is more expensive than normal grades of olive oil.

Provençal oils are rightly considered among the finest in the world. Unfortunately the production is very small, and few find their way to our markets. Keep an eye out for estate or co-operative bottled oils labelled *première pression à froid*. The label might also have *fabrication artisanale* written on it which would indicate that the traditional method was used to extract the oil. If you cannot find a single-estate olive oil, try to find an oil marked 'extra-virgin' or 'cold-pressed', if possible. A beautiful, fragrant, fruity oil is worth every penny it costs and will enhance so many salads and other dishes that it will not in the end seem to have been an extravagance.

OLIVES
The delicious, small, black and dark purple olives from Provence are not easy to find here. You can substitute the larger, black Spanish olives or the Greek Calamata olives. Invest in a *dénoyauteur* – an olive-pitter – it makes the job easy and neat. Olives can be kept in olive oil, herbs and garlic to improve their flavour.

BOUQUET GARNI
This term means a combination of bay leaf, parsley and thyme for flavouring soups, stews and sauces. If the herbs are fresh and in sprigs, they are tied with thin thread. If they are dried, they are wrapped in a piece of muslin. A piece of leek is often used to wrap around the

herbs to hold them together. Sometimes celery or fennel is added, but this will be specified in the recipes. An average bouquet garni should contain three parsley sprigs, one bay leaf and a sprig of thyme. When the dish is cooked the bouquet garni is removed.

HERBES DE PROVENCE

The most common herbs of Provence are thyme, rosemary, marjoram, fennel, oregano and bay. They are often wild and are sold mixed and dried as *herbes de Provence*. Aniseed and coriander are often included in the mixture.

Dried herbs are convenient, but personally I like to use them individually rather than pre-mixed. Dried herbs (and spices) lose their fragrance with time and it is worth checking for staleness occasionally in your dried-herb and spice cupboard.

GARLIC

Buy the fat garlic of France that begins to arrive in July. It is streaked with pink and purple and the cloves are large and juicy. Keep away from dried heads and those with tiny cloves, which are fiddly to use. Garlic that is beginning to sprout should also be avoided. If the garlic you are using has a green centre – the germ – remove it before using the clove. It has a strong bite. When garlic is roasted or braised the flavour is much milder than when minced or crushed. For centuries the French have been roasting whole cloves of garlic and enjoying the creamy contents spread on buttered toast.

If the preparation instructions for garlic specify that the clove is to be 'bruised' before chopping or crushing, simply flatten the clove with the side of a heavy knife blade, remove the skin and then continue.

TOMATOES

It is now possible to find good-flavoured tomatoes over here in the summer months. French tomatoes are a good bet, or those grown outdoors. It helps to buy them ahead of time and leave them to ripen in a warm sunny spot.

To prepare skinned, de-seeded and chopped tomatoes, first drop them one or two at a time into simmering water and leave them for 10–15 seconds. Lift them out with a slotted spoon and when they are cool enough to handle, peel off the skins. Cut them in halves and remove the seeds using your fingers. Cut out the dark stem base. Chop the flesh into small dice.

ANCHOVIES

Fresh anchovies would often be used in Provence, but these are not easy to get in the UK. Canned anchovy fillets, drained, make a good substitute, and I have assumed that these will be used for the recipes in this book.

Tomates à la Provençale (Provençal stuffed tomatoes)

Bouillabaisse with Rouille (Fish stew with rouille)

Les Sardines Grillées (Grilled sardines)

Daube de Bœuf (Provençal beef stew)

SOUPS

BOUILLABAISSE

Fish stew — Serves 8

Preparation time: 25 minutes + 1¾ hours cooking

For the fish stock:

- *1.1 kg (2½ lb) fish bones, heads, tails, etc., from white fish minus gills*
- *1 large onion, chopped*
- *25 g (1 oz) butter*
- *several sprigs of parsley, chopped roughly*
- *1 bouquet garni*
- *10 peppercorns*
- *2.75 litres (5 pints) water*

For the fish stew:

- *3 tablespoons olive oil*
- *2 shallots, chopped*
- *1 onion, chopped*
- *3 garlic cloves, crushed*
- *1 large fennel bulb, chopped*
- *a good pinch of saffron strands*
- *a strip of orange zest*
- *6 tablespoons chopped parsley*
- *1 kg (2 lb) tomatoes, quartered*
- *1 tablespoon tomato purée*
- *1.25 kg (3 lb) mixed fish fillets such as red snapper, John Dory, monkfish, red mullet, haddock or hake*

Bouillabaisse is a fragrant and delicious fish stew which is traditionally made from Mediterranean rock fish and served with rouille, a pounded chilli and garlic sauce. This anglicised version makes use of the varied fresh fish available to us in Britain.

Bouillabaisse is really a meal in itself, so you need only serve fruit or something very light to follow. It is easy to do for entertaining because it can be prepared in advance, except for the final few minutes when the fish is cooked. It is not hard to make or even that time-consuming, so do not be put off by the long list of ingredients. The rouille will taste very strong when you make it but it will be perfect when spread on toast and soaked in the soup. Buy a few whole fish for this soup and ask for them to be filleted; use the bones and a few extras for the stock. Only use heads and bones from white fish.

To make the fish stock, rinse the bones under cold water and chop them into chunks. In a large pan, soften the onion in the butter. Stir in the parsley, bouquet garni and peppercorns. Add the fish bones and stir to coat them in the butter. Add the water and slowly bring to the boil, uncovered. Simmer gently for 25 minutes, uncovered, then strain the stock and season.

To make the stew, heat the oil and gently fry the shallots, onion, garlic and fennel in a large pan. Add the saffron, orange zest and parsley and stir for a few more minutes and then add the tomatoes and tomato purée. Stir for a few more minutes and then add 2.25 litres (4 pints) of the fish stock, and season. Bring to a boil and simmer from 30–45 minutes. Sieve the soup through a fairly large-holed disc of a vegetable mill or liquidise just enough to leave some

salt and pepper

To serve:

750 g (1½ lb) small waxy potatoes, such as nicola, charlotte or pink fir apple

finely chopped fresh parsley

16 slices of bread cut from a baguette, grilled

175 ml (6 fl oz) rouille (page 19)

texture. Return the sieved soup to the pan. Taste for seasoning and add more saffron, salt or pepper as needed.

Boil the potatoes. Meanwhile, cut the fish fillets into large chunks and skin any fillet that has a rough scaly skin. Before serving, bring the soup to the boil, add the fish and boil for 5–7 minutes.

To serve: cut the potatoes into thick slices and place a few chunks in each warm soup bowl. Ladle out a few pieces of fish with some broth and arrange over the potatoes. Sprinkle with parsley. Pass the warm grilled bread and the rouille. Guests spread the bread with the rouille and drop it into the soup.

SOUPE DE TOMATE

Tomato soup — Serves 4

Preparation time: 10 minutes + 20 minutes cooking

2 tablespoons olive oil

2 shallots, chopped finely

1 celery stick, chopped finely

1 kg (2 lb) good-flavoured tomatoes, quartered

a pinch of sugar

600 ml (1 pint) chicken stock

2 tablespoons chopped basil

salt and pepper

Heat the olive oil in a large pan. Add the shallots and celery and cook gently, stirring occasionally, until the vegetables soften. Stir in the tomatoes and sugar and cook for a few minutes before adding the stock. Bring to the boil and simmer gently, covered, for 20 minutes.

Cool slightly, then sieve through the medium disc of a food mill. Alternatively the soup can be puréed in a blender or processor and then passed through a sieve. Return to the pan and reheat if serving hot; season with salt and pepper and stir in the basil. Serve hot or cold.

Variation: For cold cream of tomato soup, simply stir in the contents of a 284 ml (½ pint) carton of single cream. For hot cream of tomato soup, bring the cream to the boil in a clean pan and add the soup gradually.

Soupe de Tomate (Tomato soup)

Soupe au Pistou (Vegetable soup with pistou)

Aïgo Bouïdo (Garlic soup)

SOUPE AU PISTOU

Vegetable soup with pistou — Serves 8–10

Preparation time: 40 minutes + 8 hours soaking + 2½ hours cooking

375 g (12 oz) dried white haricot beans
2 bay leaves
1 small onion
2 litres (3½ pints) water
4 tablespoons olive oil
2 leeks, chopped
2 carrots, diced
2 potatoes, diced
500 g (1 lb) tomatoes, skinned and diced
250 g (8 oz) green beans, diced
250 g (8 oz) courgettes, diced
1 bouquet garni
1.2 litres (2 pints) boiling water
125 g (4 oz) shelled broad beans, or frozen baby broad beans
125 g (4 oz) shelled green peas, or frozen petits pois
1 quantity pistou (page 19)
salt and pepper
grilled baguette slices, to serve

In summer in Provence this soup is made with three types of fresh white beans and other vegetables. The delicious pistou – a paste made with basil, garlic and olive oil – is freshly made and added to the soup for flavouring. Fresh basil and dried white beans are readily available so the soup can be produced here all year round, and the vegetables can be altered to accommodate the seasons.

Soak the beans in water to cover for at least 8 hours or overnight. Drain the beans, then place them in a large pan with the bay leaves, onion and water. Bring to the boil and boil rapidly for at least 10 minutes; simmer for 1–1½ hours until tender. Drain and discard the bay leaves, onion and cooking liquid. Season with salt and pepper.

Heat the oil in a large pan. Add the leeks, carrots and potatoes and stir to coat in the oil. Add the tomatoes, green beans, courgettes, bouquet garni and some salt and pepper. Pour over the boiling water to cover, and simmer for 45 minutes. Add the cooked white beans, broad beans and peas and cook for a further 10–15 minutes. Stir in a few tablespoons of the pistou, taste the soup for seasoning and serve. Pass the rest of the sauce and the bread separately.

AIGO BOUIDO

Garlic soup — Serves 6–8

Preparation time: 25 minutes + 30 minutes cooking

1 whole head of garlic, separated into cloves, bruised

2 small sprigs of fresh sage

2 cloves

2 teaspoons salt

several grindings of black pepper

4 sprigs of parsley

7 tablespoons extra-virgin olive oil

2 litres (3½ pints) water

3 egg yolks

For the bread accompaniment:

24 rounds of bread cut from a baguette

a little olive oil

125 g (4 oz) grated Gruyère or parmesan cheese

The farther south you go in France the more garlic you will find is used in cooking. This is partly because the garlic often has a gentler flavour when grown in a hot climate. This soup is perfect for even the stronger varieties of garlic because when garlic is simmered its flavour is transformed. If you did not know, you would never guess what this aromatic soup was made of.

Preheat the oven to Gas Mark 3/160°C/325°F. In a large pan combine the garlic, sage, cloves, salt, pepper, parsley and 3 tablespoons of olive oil with the water. Bring to the boil and simmer for 20 minutes.

Meanwhile, place the rounds of bread in one layer on a baking sheet. Bake for 25 minutes, turning them over once during that time to dry them out. Preheat the grill. Brush them with olive oil and cover with a layer of the cheese; dribble a bit of olive oil over the top. Place them under the grill until the cheese has melted and lightly browned (about 5 minutes). Keep them warm in a low oven while you finish the soup.

Strain the soup into a bowl, pressing as much of the juices out of the ingredients as you can. Rinse the pan and pour the strained broth back into it.

Whisk the egg yolks in a bowl until thick. Slowly, drop by drop, whisk in the remaining 4 tablespoons of olive oil until you have a thick cream. Reheat the soup. Whisk a few ladlefuls of hot soup into the egg yolk mixture. While whisking, pour the thinned egg yolk mixture back into the soup. Keep the soup below boiling point. Place a few rounds of the toasted cheese bread in individual soup bowls. Ladle some soup over the bread and serve. Serve any remaining bread separately.

BOURRIDE

Fish soup Serves 8

Preparation time: 50 minutes + 50 minutes cooking

- *750 g (1½ lb) extra white fish heads and bones*
- *1 leek, chopped*
- *1 large onion, chopped,*
- *1 carrot, chopped*
- *2 strips of orange zest*
- *1 teaspoon dried fennel seeds*
- *1 teaspoon dried thyme*
- *2 bay leaves*
- *3 sprigs of parsley*
- *300 ml (½ pint) dry white wine*
- *2.25 litres (4 pints) water*
- *1.75 kg (4 lb) mixture of whole fish such as whiting, grey mullet, sea bream or tail end of halibut, filleted, with bones reserved*
- *300 ml (½ pint) aïoli (page 18)*
- *2 egg yolks*
- *salt and pepper*
- *16 rounds of bread cut from a baguette and dried out in a moderate oven for 25 minutes, to serve*

Bourride is a lovely creamy fish soup traditionally flavoured with aïoli, the garlicky mayonnaise. It does not rely on Mediterranean fish so it can be made very successfully with fish such as halibut, whiting and grey mullet. It is quite substantial and perfect for a special lunch when you need only serve a salad and dessert to follow.

Place all the fish bones and heads in a large pan. Add the leek, onion, carrot, orange zest, fennel seeds, thyme, bay leaves and parsley. Pour over the wine and water and bring to the boil. Skim off any scum that floats to the surface. Simmer for 40 minutes.

Strain through a sieve into a large clean pan, pressing against the vegetables and bones to extract as much flavour as possible. You should now have approximately 2.25 litres (4 pints) of stock. Bring the broth to the boil, add the fish fillets and simmer very gently for 10 minutes. Remove the fish with a slotted spoon to a large, heated soup tureen or platter, and cover loosely with foil. Keep the broth hot over a very low heat.

Place half of the aïoli in a medium-sized bowl and stir in the egg yolks. Whisk several ladlefuls of hot broth into the aïoli, one at a time, being sure that each ladleful is blended in before adding the next. Pour the aïoli mixture into the broth and heat to just below simmering point. Take great care not to boil the soup or it will curdle. Season with salt and pepper. Pour over the fish in the tureen or place some fish in individual bowls and pour the broth over. Serve the soup with the toast and remaining aïoli separately.

SOUPE DE LENTILLES

Lentil soup Serves 10–12

Preparation time: 15 minutes + 1½ hours cooking

500 g (1 lb) puy, green or brown lentils

2 tablespoons olive oil

175 g (6 oz) onions, chopped

1 garlic clove, chopped

175 g (6 oz) potatoes, peeled and diced

2 litres (3½ pints) chicken, duck or game stock

1 bouquet garni

375 g (12 oz) sorrel or spinach

lemon juice, if necessary

salt and pepper

300 ml (½ pint) soured cream or crème fraîche, to serve

Pick over the lentils for any stones and rinse in cold water. Heat the olive oil in a large pan, add the onions, garlic and potatoes and stir for several minutes to soften the onions. Add the lentils and stir to coat in the oil, then add the stock and bouquet garni. Cover and simmer for at least 1¼ hours, or until the lentils are soft. Check during cooking to see if there is enough liquid, and top up with water as necessary.

Pull off and discard any coarse stems from the sorrel or spinach and chop finely. Add the spinach or sorrel to the soup and season well with salt and pepper. Simmer, uncovered, for another 10 minutes.

If you are using spinach, add a few tablespoons of lemon juice to the soup. Remove the bouquet garni and either serve the soup as it is, sieve it through the medium disc of a vegetable mill, or process it just enough to leave some texture. Add a dollop of cream to each serving.

SAUCES

AIOLI

Garlic mayonnaise — Makes 450 ml (¾ pint)

Preparation time: 15 minutes

4–6 garlic cloves

2 egg yolks, at room temperature

½ teaspoon salt

250 ml (8 fl oz) olive oil

2–3 tablespoons lemon juice

pepper

Mistral, the Provençal poet, wrote 'Aïoli intoxicates gently, fills the body with warmth, and the soul with enthusiasm. In its essence it concentrates the strength, the gaiety, of the Provençal sunshine.'

This garlicky mayonnaise must be made in the traditional way in order to obtain the thick texture that a true aïoli should have. The strength and pungency of garlic can vary enormously, so start with the smaller amount – you can always add more later. The sauce has a strong olive oil flavour too, but if you prefer, substitute sunflower oil for some of the olive oil. It is wonderful as a dip or with boiled potatoes or fish.

Cut the garlic cloves in half. If they have a green sprout in the middle, discard it. Place the garlic in a mortar or bowl. Pound with a pestle or the back of a spoon until you have a smooth paste, then add the egg yolks and salt. Pound until the mixture is thick and well blended. Change over to a whisk and stir in the oil, drop by drop. Once you have a thick creamy mixture you can incorporate the oil a bit faster – much like making an ordinary mayonnaise. Add the lemon juice and thin with a tablespoon of water if the sauce is too dense. Add some pepper and taste for seasoning, adding extra garlic if necessary.

ROUILLE

Makes 175 ml (6 fl oz)

Preparation time: 15 minutes

½ red pepper, de-seeded (optional)

½–1 chilli, de-seeded and chopped

2–4 garlic cloves, crushed

a large pinch of saffron strands

1 slice bread, crust removed

2 egg yolks

175 ml (6 fl oz) olive oil

salt

This sauce always accompanies bouillabaisse (page 10), but it can also give character to other soups.

If you are using the red pepper, blanch it in boiling water for a few minutes and drain. Chop roughly and place in a mortar or food processor with the chilli, garlic and saffron. Pound or blend to a paste. Soak the bread in water and squeeze dry. Add the bread and egg yolks and some salt to the mortar or processor. Pound or blend until all the ingredients are blended. Whisk or blend in the oil, drop by drop, until the mixture is thick and creamy.

PISTOU

Basil, garlic and parmesan sauce — Makes 250 ml (8 fl oz)

Preparation time: 15 minutes

3–4 garlic cloves

a pinch of salt

25–30 large basil leaves, shredded

50 g (2 oz) freshly grated parmesan cheese

175 ml (6 fl oz) olive oil

This is the sauce to make in the summer months when basil is plentiful. It is delicious with pasta or as a dip for vegetables and is a most useful addition to soups. Garlic varies in strength, so adjust the amount according to how fiery yours is.

Crush the garlic in a mortar with a pestle or in a bowl with the back of a spoon, until it becomes a paste. Add salt and the basil leaves and continue to pound to a paste. Transfer to a bowl and add the cheese. Slowly stir in the oil until smooth. Alternatively you can make the sauce in a blender or food processor: put in the garlic, basil, salt, cheese and oil and blend for a few seconds. Stir with a long-handled spoon and blend again. Repeat until you have a smooth paste.

TAPENADE

Olive and anchovy spread — Makes 400 ml (14 fl oz)

Preparation time: 5 minutes

- *1 garlic clove, crushed*
- *175 g (6 oz) black Calamata olives, stoned*
- *6 anchovy fillets, drained and chopped*
- *2 tablespoons capers*
- *4 tablespoons olive oil*
- *125 g (4 oz) lightmeat tuna in soya oil, drained*
- *pepper*

This is a fragrant, salty spread that can be used as a dip for raw vegetables or be spread on croûtes – toasted slices of bread. It can be used to stuff hard-boiled eggs and is excellent with grilled chicken.

Purée all the ingredients in a blender or food processor. Taste for seasoning and add more of any of the ingredients that you fancy.

ANCHOIADE

Anchovy spread — Makes approx. 250 ml (8 fl oz)

Preparation time: 20 minutes

- *50 g (2 oz) can of anchovies in olive oil*
- *2–3 garlic cloves, unpeeled*
- *1 egg yolk*
- *1 tablespoon cider vinegar*
- *150 ml (1/4 pint) olive oil*

Though often used as a spread on toast, anchoïade can be served with boiled potatoes or fish. It can also be stirred into tomato soup or fish soups in place of rouille. It is delicious as a stuffing for hard-boiled eggs or with baked potatoes or cold beef.

Drain the anchovies and reserve the oil. Chop the anchovies roughly and place in a mortar or bowl. Crush the garlic with the side of a knife blade, remove the skin and add the garlic to the anchovies. Use a pestle or wooden spoon and crush to a paste. Whisk in the egg yolk and vinegar. Whisk in the reserved anchovy oil as well as the olive oil, drop by drop, until the mixture is thick and well-blended. The consistency should be thick, like a mayonnaise. Turn into a bowl and refrigerate, covered, if not serving immediateiy.

Pistou (Basil, garlic and parmesan sauce)
Anchoïade (Anchovy spread)
Tapenade (Olive and anchovy spread)

FIRST COURSES AND LIGHT MEALS

MOULES MARINIERE

Mussels with wine, shallots and parsley — Serves 6

Preparation and cooking time: 45 minutes

2.75 kg (6 lb) mussels

4 shallots, chopped finely

300 ml (½ pint) dry white wine

25 g (1 oz) butter

4 tablespoons parsley, chopped finely

crusty French bread, to serve

Don't be daunted by the prospect of serving mussels at home. They are inexpensive, easy to prepare and cook in a matter of minutes. This is the classic French way of serving them – simple and delicious.

Scrub the mussels with a stiff brush and scrape off any barnacles. Let the mussels rest in cold salted water. Change the water at intervals if it becomes muddy. Discard any with broken shells or that are open. Remove the beards just before cooking the mussels.

Using a large pan with a tight-fitting lid, bring the shallots and wine to the boil. Add the mussels, cover and cook over a high heat, shaking the pan occasionally, for about 5 minutes or until the mussels have just opened. Do not overcook them or they will become tough. Discard any that do not open.

Strain the liquor through a muslin-lined sieve set over a pan. Using a slotted spoon, place the mussels in a large heated tureen or bowl. Heat the liquor and whisk in the butter; pour over the mussels and scatter the mussels with the parsley. Ladle into 6 warmed soup plates and serve with crusty bread.

PISSALADIERE

Niçoise onion tart — Serves 6–8

Preparation time: 15 minutes + 1½ hours rising + 1 hour cooking

For the dough:

200 g (7 oz) plain or strong white flour

1 teaspoon salt

¾ teaspoon easy-blend dried yeast

75 ml (3 fl oz) tepid water

1 small egg (size 5–6)

For the topping:

4 tablespoons olive oil

1 kg (2 lb) mild onions, sliced

1 teaspoon fresh or dried thyme

4 tomatoes, skinned and sliced

50 g (2 oz) can of anchovy fillets, drained

6 sun-dried tomatoes in seasoned oil, drained and cut into slivers (optional)

12 small black olives, stoned

salt and pepper

The name for this succulent onion tart comes from 'pissala', a purée of tiny fish preserved in brine which is sometimes still used in place of the more usual anchovies. Pissaladière is a cross between a quiche and a pizza and is made with either a bread dough or an ordinary pie pastry.

To make the dough, place the flour and salt in a bowl and mix in the yeast. Add the water and egg and stir together until the mixture forms a mass. Turn the dough out onto a floured board and knead until soft and smooth, adding a bit more flour if the dough is too sticky. Place in a greased bowl, cover with a damp cloth and leave to rise in a warm place for 1 hour or until doubled in size, while you prepare the topping.

To make the topping, heat the oil in a heavy frying-pan; add the onions, thyme and some salt and pepper. Cover and cook over a very low heat for 25 minutes. Remove the lid and continue to cook, stirring occasionally, until the onions are golden and very soft – almost a purée.

When the dough has risen, punch it down and roll out on a floured surface. Place in an oiled 30 cm (12-inch) pie or pizza pan and stretch it out so that the crust is slightly higher on the sides. Spoon the onions onto the dough. Arrange the tomatoes on top and make a lattice pattern with the anchovies and sun-dried tomatoes, if using. Place olives in the gaps. Leave to rise for at least 30 minutes. Place a baking sheet in the centre of the oven and preheat the oven to Gas Mark 5/190°C/375°F. Bake on the hot baking sheet for 30 minutes. Serve warm.

Moules Marinière (Mussels with wine, shallots and parsley)

Les Poivrons au Four (Grilled peppers)

Pissaladière (Niçoise onion tart)

LES POIVRONS AU FOUR

Grilled peppers — Serves 6

Preparation time: 10 minutes + 15 minutes cooking

- *3 large red peppers*
- *3 large yellow peppers*
- *4 tablespoons extra-virgin olive oil*
- *3 tablespoons capers, drained*
- *salt and pepper*
- *several anchovy fillets (optional)*

Not only is the flavour of peppers greatly enhanced by grilling but they are also far more digestible. The only trouble is that they are so delicious you will find that everyone asks for more.

Preheat the grill to its highest heat. Grill the peppers until the skins are well blackened and blistered. Turn them over so that all sides get charred. Place the peppers in a polythene bag and leave to cool for 5 minutes – this enables the skins to be removed more easily. Remove one pepper at a time from the bag, wet your fingers with cold water and pull off the charred skins. Peel the other peppers in the same way. Cut open the peppers, remove and discard the core and seeds. Cut the peppers into strips. Place in a shallow dish along with any juices you can save. Pour over the olive oil and season with salt and pepper. Scatter the capers over the top, and the anchovies if you are using them. Serve warm with good crusty bread.

CRUDITES AND BAGNA CAUDA

Raw vegetables and warm sauce — Serves 8

Preparation time: 20 minutes + 5 minutes cooking

- *Little Gem lettuce, leaves separated*
- *watercress, coarse stems removed*
- *chicory, leaves separated*
- *cauliflower, florets separated*
- *celery sticks*

This is really a fondue; guests dip raw vegetables in a communal bowl of hot sauce made from anchovies, garlic and olive oil. You can go to town on the number of raw vegetables you use for this dish. Pick the freshest you can find and choose a variety of colours to make the dish a feast for the eyes. The ingredients list gives you some ideas for your selection.

Arrange two platters with a mixture of some of the vegetables, as suggested, from the list.

spring onions, whole or sliced lengthways

young spinach leaves

cucumber, peeled, de-seeded and cut into sticks

fennel bulbs, cut into thin wedges

radishes, whole with leaves intact

mushrooms, halved

carrots, cut into sticks

courgettes, cut into sticks

cherry tomatoes

red, green and yellow peppers, de-seeded and cut into sticks

young asparagus, pared

fresh broad beans, shelled

mange tout

For the sauce:

3 slices of white bread, crusts removed

4 tablespoons milk

50 g (2 oz) can of anchovy fillets, drained and chopped

2 garlic cloves, chopped

250 ml (8 fl oz) olive oil

25 g (1 oz) butter

1 tablespoon red wine vinegar

salt and pepper

Soak the bread in the milk until saturated. Squeeze out the excess milk and place the bread in a blender or food processor. Add the anchovies and garlic, and purée. Slowly add the olive oil to make a smooth paste, and season with pepper.

Heat the butter in a pan set over a low heat, add the paste and vinegar and heat until warm but not hot. Season with pepper and salt if necessary. Place in a flameproof dish and keep warm on a hot-plate. It will separate, but as guests dip into it they will stir it up.

Guests serve themselves by choosing a selection of the vegetables and dipping them, either with their fingers or a fork, into the warm sauce. Serve with good crusty bread.

ARTICHAUTS A LA BARIGOULE

'Barigoule' stuffed artichokes — Serves 4

Preparation time: 1 hour + 55 minutes cooking

4 large fresh artichokes

juice of one lemon, plus extra to taste

3 tablespoons olive oil

1 carrot, chopped very finely

1 celery stick, chopped finely

2 shallots, chopped finely

1 garlic clove, chopped finely

150 ml (¼ pint) white wine

300 ml (½ pint) chicken stock

1 bay leaf

salt and pepper

For the stuffing:

15 g (½ oz) butter

1 tablespoon olive oil

100 g (3½ oz) unsmoked streaky bacon, chopped

1 shallot, chopped finely

250 g (8 oz) mushrooms, chopped finely

3 tablespoons breadcrumbs

2 tablespoons mixed chopped parsley, tarragon or chives

salt and pepper

Artichauts à la Barigoule ('Barigoule' stuffed artichokes)

In Provence the word 'barigoulo' means morel mushroom. Perhaps originally morels were used in the stuffing, but in today's France ordinary mushrooms are what you are likely to find. Although preparing the artichokes is a bit fiddly, they do provide a special first course.

To prepare the artichokes, snap off the stems at the base, then break off the two lower rows of leaves. Slice off the top third of the artichoke using a very sharp knife. Open out the inner middle leaves with your fingers. To remove the hairy choke, first cut all around the choke with a knife, then scoop out the choke using a long-handled teaspoon. As each artichoke is prepared, drop it into a large bowl of cold water to which the juice of one lemon has been added.

To make the stuffing, heat the butter and oil in a frying-pan. Lightly brown the bacon, then add the shallot and mushrooms and continue frying until lightly coloured. Mix in the breadcrumbs and herbs, and season. Stuff the drained artichoke cups with the mixture. Tie a string around the leaves of each artichoke to keep the leaves in place.

Use a covered flameproof casserole or pan which is wide and deep enough to hold the artichokes upright. Heat 2 tablespoons of the olive oil and fry the carrot, celery, shallots and garlic gently, stirring, until soft and lightly coloured. Set the artichokes on top. Pour in the wine and stock and dribble the remaining olive oil over the artichokes. Season with salt and pepper and add the bay leaf. Cover and simmer very gently for 45 minutes, or until the artichokes are tender when the base is pierced with a fork. Baste the artichokes with the liquids in the pan a few times and add a little water, if needed, during the cooking time.

Remove the artichokes from the pan and place them on a heated serving platter. Remove the strings. Season the cooking juices and vegetables with lemon juice and salt and pepper. Pour into a jug and serve separately.

GNOCCHI DE POMMES DE TERRE

Potato gnocchi — Serves 6 as a first course

Preparation time: 25 minutes + 1¼ hours cooking

For the sauce:

1.05 kg (2¼ lb) good-flavoured tomatoes, quartered

3 tablespoons olive oil

2 shallots, chopped finely

1 small celery stick, chopped finely

a pinch of sugar

salt and pepper

For the gnocchi:

500 g (1 lb) large baking potatoes

25 g (1 oz) butter

1 egg, beaten

75–100 g (3–3½ oz) plain flour

50 g (2 oz) parmesan cheese, grated

a little fresh nutmeg

1 tablespoon sunflower oil

salt and pepper

freshly grated parmesan cheese, to serve

Because Italy is a neighbour of Provence, it is not surprising that many Italian dishes have slipped across the border and have become part of Provençal cuisine. The name 'gnocchi' comes from the Provençal word 'inhocs' so this may in fact be a case of Italy adapting itself most successfully to a French invention.

To make the gnocchi, preheat the oven to Gas Mark 6/200°C/400°F and bake the potatoes for 1 hour, or until very tender.

Meanwhile, to make the sauce, place all the ingredients in a pan, cover and simmer until the vegetables are tender (about 15 minutes). Push through a sieve into a clean pan and taste for seasoning.

Wearing an oven glove, cut the potatoes in half and scoop out the insides into a shallow bowl. This will allow some of the steam to evaporate and will help to dry out the potatoes. While the potatoes are still hot, purée them with a potato masher or food mill. Beat in the butter and the egg. Sift the flour and beat in just enough to make a dough that is soft and smooth and just slightly sticky. Beat in the cheese and the nutmeg. Season with salt and pepper. Leave to cool.

With floured hands, break off pieces of the dough and form sausage-like rolls about 2.5 cm (1 inch) thick. Cut the rolls into 2.5 cm (1 inch) lengths. With a fork, gently dent the middles of the gnocchi, to help them cook evenly. Lay the gnocchi on plates, covered with clean tea towels.

Bring a large pan of water to the boil, add 1 tablespoon of salt and the sunflower oil. Cook the gnocchi very gently in batches for 3 minutes. Do not overcook or they will fall apart. Lift them out with a slotted spoon and place on a heated serving dish. Pour over the sauce and serve with some grated parmesan passed separately.

SOCCA

Chick-pea pancakes — Makes 8–10 pancakes

Preparation time: 25 minutes + 20 minutes standing + 15 minutes cooking

200 g (7 oz) chick-pea or gram flour

65 g (2½ oz) plain flour

400 ml (14 fl oz) warm water

2 tablespoons olive oil, plus extra for cooking

½ teaspoon dried thyme

salt and pepper

Socca is a speciality from around the Marseilles area. Pieces of socca, a large savoury pancake made from chick-pea flour, are sold hot at the street markets wrapped in paper. This version makes thinner pancakes which are delicious with tapenade (page 20) or herbed goat's cheese.

Sift the two flours together. Add the water and beat until smooth. Add the oil and thyme, and season with salt and pepper. Let the batter stand for 20 minutes.

Heat a lightly oiled 23 cm (9-inch) heavy frying-pan over a medium heat. When the pan is quite hot, pour in a small ladleful (4 table-spoons) of the batter. Quickly tip and rotate the pan to spread the batter thinly. Cook for 30 seconds, then turn over with a spatula and cook for 15 seconds more, or until the pancake begins to dry out on the underside. Transfer to a warm plate and keep warm in a low oven. Repeat the process until all the batter is used up, oiling the pan as necessary. Serve warm with any savoury filling.

Gnocchi de Pommes de Terre (Potato gnocchi)

Socca (Chick-pea pancakes)

Légumes au Four (Baked vegetables)

LEGUMES AU FOUR

Baked vegetables — Serves 8

Preparation time: 15 minutes + 50 minutes cooking

- *2–3 aubergines*
- *1 kg (2 lb) courgettes*
- *6 tomatoes*
- *3 red onions*
- *2 red peppers*
- *2 yellow peppers*
- *16 small waxy potatoes*
- *extra-virgin olive oil*
- *salt*
- *grilled bread or warmed crusty bread, to serve*

The fragrant Mediterranean vegetables that we associate with Provence are at their best in this very simple recipe. It is so good that I have it on my list of favourite dishes. It can be served as a first course or a light meal accompanied by grilled or good fresh crusty bread.

Preheat the oven to Gas Mark 7/220°C/450°F.

Wash and dry the vegetables, leaving the skins on all but the onions. Cut them into large chunks; the courgettes, onions and peppers in 4 pieces, the potatoes and tomatoes in half, and the aubergines in 4 or 6 pieces. Make a few slashes in the exposed flesh of the aubergines, sprinkle with salt and, after about 5 minutes, squeeze out some of the moisture.

Divide the vegetables between 2 baking sheets, spreading them out in one layer. Sprinkle them quite lavishly with salt and then pour over a good bit of olive oil. Toss the vegetables with your hands so that they become well covered with the oil and salt and spread them out again over the sheets.

Bake for about 50 minutes. You will know that they are done when the potatoes are cooked through and the other vegetables are soft and beginning to brown. You can give them a few minutes under a grill if you like them to be more charred. Arrange a sample of all the vegetables on individual plates. They are quite delicious warm and are also good at room temperature.

CAVIAR PROVENCALE

Aubergine caviar — Makes approx. 900 ml (1½ pints)

Preparation time: 5 minutes + 30 minutes cooking

- *1 kg (2 lb) aubergines, stalks removed*
- *200 g (7 oz) shelled walnuts*
- *1–2 garlic cloves, chopped very finely*
- *a few shakes of Tabasco sauce*
- *½ teaspoon grated fresh root ginger (optional)*
- *6–8 tablespoons olive oil*
- *salt and pepper*

This is a quite delectable spread and perfect too for vegetarians. Serve it with toast as a first course or as an appetiser with drinks. It will keep if refrigerated for up to a week.

Preheat the oven to Gas Mark 7/220°C/425°F. Place the aubergines in a shallow baking dish or tin and bake for about 30 minutes, or until they are tender. Cut in half and scoop out the flesh.

Grind the walnuts in a blender or food processor. Add the aubergine flesh and blend until it forms a smooth purée. Add the garlic, Tabasco and ginger if using and process until combined. With the food processor or blender running, slowly drizzle in the oil until you have a creamy, thick mixture. Season with salt and pepper.

CELERI REMOULADE

Celeriac in mustard sauce — Serves 6–8

Preparation time: 15 minutes + 30 minutes standing

- *2 teaspoons lemon juice*
- *1½ teaspoons salt*
- *500–625 g (1–1¼ lb) celeriac*
- *2 tablespoons Dijon mustard*
- *1 egg yolk*
- *150 ml (¼ pint) olive oil (or half olive oil and half sunflower oil)*
- *1 tablespoon white wine vinegar*

In every corner of France you will find this tasty dish of shredded raw celery root robed in a mustard sauce. It is simple to do and is a delicious first course.

Place the lemon juice and salt in a bowl. Coarsely grate the celeriac. Immediately toss in the bowl with the salt and lemon juice. Leave for 30 minutes.

Meanwhile, warm another bowl in hot water and dry it. Add the mustard and egg yolk and whisk together to blend. Whisk in the oil, drop by drop. After about a quarter of the oil has been added, the rest can be poured in more quickly. This could also be done in a food

salt and pepper

2 tablespoons finely chopped parsley, to garnish

processor or blender: pour the oil in a slow, steady stream with the motor running. Add the vinegar and salt and pepper to taste.

Rinse the celeriac in cold water and drain it. Dry in a clean towel or on kitchen paper. Fold it into the dressing and taste for seasoning. Fold in the parsley or garnish individual servings with it.

This can be served at once but it will be more tender if it is chilled for a few hours. It will keep for several days, covered, in the refrigerator.

POIVRONS AU GRUYERE

Open sandwiches of peppers, cheese and anchovies — Serves 4

Preparation time: 10 minutes + 15 minutes cooking

50 g (2 oz) can of anchovies in olive oil

1 garlic clove

2 teaspoons wine vinegar

6–7 tablespoons extra-virgin olive oil

3 red peppers

4 slices of good white crusty bread, cut from a large loaf

125 g (4 oz) Gruyère cheese, sliced thinly

olive oil

salt and pepper

A very tasty way to start a meal.

Preheat the grill. Drain the anchovies and reserve the oil. Chop the anchovies roughly and place in a mortar or bowl. Add the garlic and some pepper. Use a pestle or wooden spoon and crush to a paste. Stir in the vinegar and slowly, by droplets, stir in the olive oil until you have a thick sauce. Taste for seasoning.

Place the peppers under the grill until they are charred on all sides. Turn them once or twice so that they will blacken evenly. Place the peppers in a polythene bag. Leave to cool for 5 minutes, then remove one pepper at a time from the bag and peel off the skin with your fingers. Cut the peppers into 4 pieces lengthways and remove the core and seeds. Place the peppers on an oiled baking sheet, skin side up, and sprinkle lightly with salt and olive oil.

At the same time grill the bread on both sides. Spread a layer of the anchovy paste on the bread, and arrange 3 pepper pieces in one layer on top. Place a slice of cheese over each pepper and set under the grill until the cheese melts. The open sandwiches can be cut into 3 pieces to make a nicer presentation, if desired.

Papeton de Aubergines (Aubergine and vegetable mould)
Poivrons au Gruyère (Open sandwiches of peppers, cheese and anchovies)

PAPETON D'AUBERGINES

Aubergine and vegetable mould — Serves 6–8

Preparation time: 40 minutes + 1½ hours cooking

- *3 aubergines*
- *6 tablespoons olive oil*
- *300 g (10 oz) courgettes, cut into 1 cm (½-inch) slices*
- *1 large mild onion, chopped*
- *2 garlic cloves, chopped*
- *1 red pepper, diced*
- *1 green pepper, diced*
- *375 g (12 oz) tomatoes, skinned, de-seeded and chopped*
- *4 tablespoons finely chopped fresh parsley*
- *1 egg*
- *50 g (2 oz) breadcrumbs*
- *salt and pepper*

Aubergines, courgettes, peppers and onions are baked in a mould lined with the dark skins of the aubergines. A beautiful summer starter or light lunch.

Preheat the oven to Gas Mark 6/200°C/400°F.

Cut the aubergines in half, make a few slits with a knife in the flesh and brush with a little of the olive oil. Place on a baking sheet, cut-side down, and bake for about 15–20 minutes, until the flesh has softened. Scoop out the flesh, being careful not to pierce the skins. Chop the flesh and reserve the skins.

Meanwhile sprinkle the courgettes with salt and leave in a colander to drain for 15 minutes. Rinse the courgettes and pat dry with kitchen paper. Heat 1½ tablespoons of the oil in a large frying-pan and brown the courgettes. Remove them from the pan. Add another 1½ tablespoons of the oil and cook the onion and garlic until they begin to soften. Add the peppers, aubergine flesh, courgettes, tomatoes and parsley to the pan. Season well with salt and pepper. Cook, uncovered for about 8–10 minutes, or until the vegetables lose some of their moisture and the mixture thickens. Remove from the heat and cool. Lightly beat the egg and add it to the vegetables, then stir in the breadcrumbs.

Preheat the oven to Gas Mark 4/180°C/350°F. Generously oil a 1.5-litre (2½-pint) charlotte mould or soufflé dish. Line the sides of the mould with the aubergine skins shiny-side out, and spoon in the vegetable mixture. Place the mould in a roasting tin and fill with enough very hot water to come one-third of the way up the mould. Bake for 45 minutes if the mould is metal and 1 hour if it is china. Leave to cool before turning out on to a serving dish. Serve at room temperature.

AUBERGINES FARCIES AUX ANCHOIS

Aubergines stuffed with anchovies — Serves 6

Preparation time: 40 minutes + 1 hour cooking

- *3 large aubergines*
- *8 anchovies, rinsed, dried and chopped finely*
- *10 black olives, chopped*
- *a small bunch of parsley, chopped finely*
- *1 tablespoon capers, drained*
- *2 garlic cloves, chopped finely*
- *100 g (3½ oz) fresh breadcrumbs*
- *4–6 tablespoons milk*
- *150 ml (¼ pint) olive oil*
- *salt and pepper*

These are substantial enough for a light lunch.

Preheat the oven to Gas Mark 3/160°C/325°F.

Halve the aubergines lengthways. Scoop out half the flesh, leaving enough to make firm shells. Arrange these in an oiled, shallow, ovenproof dish.

Chop the cut-out flesh and mix with the anchovies, olives, parsley, capers and garlic. Mix the breadcrumbs with just enough milk to make a crumbly paste and add to the other ingredients. Season only with pepper.

Sprinkle the inside of the aubergine shells with salt and divide the stuffing between them. Pour the oil over the aubergines. Bake in the preheated oven for 1 hour. Serve hot.

BROUILLADE DE TOMATES AU BASILIC

Scrambled eggs with tomato and basil — Serves 4

Preparation time: 15 minutes + 15 minutes cooking

- *3 tablespoons olive oil*
- *4 tomatoes, skinned, de-seeded and chopped*
- *a small pinch of sugar*
- *3 garlic cloves, bruised*
- *a small pinch of freeze-dried fines herbes*
- *8 eggs*
- *4–5 tablespoons shredded fresh basil leaves*
- *25 g (1 oz) butter*
- *salt and pepper*

These scrambled eggs are quite delicious and are perfect for brunch or a light lunch. Cook them slowly so that they stay creamy and soft, and serve on or with some crusty grilled bread.

Heat the oil in a heavy frying-pan and add the tomatoes, sugar, garlic and herbs. Cook over a moderate heat, stirring until the tomato juices have evaporated. Remove and discard the garlic and season the tomatoes.

Meanwhile lightly whisk the eggs, and season. Pour the eggs over the tomatoes, lower the heat and cook very gently, stirring constantly with a wooden spoon until the eggs have formed soft curds. Add the basil when the eggs are almost done. Remove from the heat and stir in the butter, cut up small. Serve at once.

RATATOUILLE

Stewed aubergine, courgettes, peppers, onions and tomatoes Serves 8

Preparation time: 35 minutes + 30 minutes standing + 50 minutes cooking

- *500 g (1 lb) aubergines*
- *500 g (1 lb) courgettes*
- *100 ml (3½ fl oz) olive oil*
- *500 g (1 lb) mild onions, sliced*
- *3 yellow or green peppers, sliced into 8 mm (⅜-inch) strips*
- *4 garlic cloves, bruised and chopped finely*
- *750 g (1½ lb) tomatoes, skinned, de-seeded and chopped*
- *4 tablespoons finely chopped fresh parsley*
- *salt and pepper*

Perhaps this is the best known of all the Provençal dishes. Cooking the vegetables separately at first helps them to retain their own character and the end result is a harmony of flavours.

Peel the aubergines and cut into 8 mm (⅜-inch) lengthways slices, then cut the slices into 8 mm (⅜-inch) strips. Leave the courgettes unpeeled but slice them into the same-sized strips. Place the aubergines and courgettes in colanders, sprinkle with salt, weigh down with small plates and weights and leave to drain for 30 minutes. Rinse under cold water and pat dry with kitchen paper.

Heat 3 tablespoons of the olive oil in a frying-pan and fry the aubergines for about 1 minute on each side. Transfer with a slotted spoon to a large bowl, and repeat with the courgettes. Add half the remaining oil and cook the onions and peppers slowly for about 10 minutes; stir in the garlic and season to taste. Transfer to the bowl. Add the remaining oil to the pan and stir in the tomatoes and parsley. Cook briskly for a few minutes to evaporate some of the moisture. Season with salt and pepper.

Place a layer of tomatoes in a heavy flameproof casserole, then add layers of the other vegetables ending with a layer of tomatoes. Cover and simmer over a low heat for 10 minutes. Baste the vegetables with the juices and correct the seasoning. Turn up the heat and cook, uncovered, for about 20 minutes. Serve hot or cold.

PIPERADE

Eggs with peppers and tomatoes — Serves 4

Preparation time: 40 minutes

- *3 tablespoons olive oil*
- *1 large mild onion, chopped*
- *3 red or green peppers or a mixture, de-seeded and cut into strips*
- *750 g (1½ lb) tomatoes, skinned, de-seeded and chopped*
- *2 garlic cloves, chopped finely*
- *1 chilli (optional), chopped finely*
- *6 eggs*
- *salt and pepper*
- *crusty bread, to serve*

This is a well-known and tasty Provençal dish which includes the favourite Mediterranean combination of tomatoes and peppers. For a more substantial dish, serve the Piperade on grilled or fried slices of gammon.

Heat the oil in a large frying-pan, add the onion and cook gently until it begins to colour. Add the peppers and continue to cook over a low heat for another 10 minutes, then add the tomatoes, garlic, chilli if using and seasoning. Raise the heat and cook until the tomato juices have thickened (about 5 minutes). Mix the eggs, season lightly, and stir them into the tomatoes. Reduce the heat to low and cook the eggs, stirring constantly, until they are creamy and set (about 4–6 minutes). Serve immediately with good crusty bread.

PATES A L'AIL

Fresh pasta with garlic sauce — Serves 4

Preparation time: 5 minutes + 30 minutes cooking

- *1 large head of fresh garlic*
- *25 g (1 oz) unsalted butter*
- *142 ml (¼ pint) carton of whipping cream*
- *375 g (12 oz) fresh tagliatelle*
- *8 sun-dried tomatoes in seasoned oil, sliced*
- *salt and pepper*

The amount of garlic in this recipe may seem enormous but when garlic is braised, its flavour mellows and the result is a most delicious pasta sauce.

Separate the cloves of garlic and place in a small pan of simmering water. Leave for 30 seconds, then drain. Place the cloves on a chopping board, cut a sliver off the base and slip off the skins.

Place the peeled garlic with the butter in a small, heavy-based pan and simmer over a low heat for 10–15 minutes, until very tender. The cloves should not colour more than a creamy yellow. Add the cream, some salt and pepper.

and simmer over a low heat for 5–10 minutes. Remove from the heat and crush the garlic with a potato masher or fork, until you have a creamy purée. Keep the sauce warm.

Cook the tagliatelle according to the packet instructions. Drain, but do not overdrain or shake the colander. Turn it into a heated bowl. Pour over the garlic sauce and tomatoes. Toss together and serve.

PAN BAGNA

'Bathed bread' Provençal sandwich — Serves 1

Preparation time: 10 minutes + 1 hour chilling

- *1 piece of baguette or a petit pain or bap, sliced in half lengthways*
- *1 garlic clove*
- *1 tablespoon olive oil*
- *a few drops of wine vinegar*
- *several slices of mild onion*
- *1 tomato, sliced*
- *½ hard-boiled egg, sliced*
- *a few strips of red or green pepper*
- *4–5 black olives*
- *a few anchovy fillets*
- *1 tablespoon canned tuna*
- *a few basil leaves*
- *salt and pepper*

This sandwich originated from the habit of using day-old bread to soak up the juices and oil from Salade Niçoise (page 70). It was so delicious that the resulting sandwich was invented and christened 'bathed bread' because of the way the juices soak into the bread. In and around Nice a special large soft roll about 20 cm (8 inches) across is baked just for pan bagna, but in other parts of Provence a piece of baguette is used. Prepare a few hours before serving.

Scoop out some of the white part of the bread and rub the inside with the garlic. Sprinkle both pieces with olive oil, vinegar, and salt and pepper. Pile the other ingredients on to one piece and sandwich with the other.

Cover tightly with clingfilm, then weigh the sandwich down with a heavy plate so that the juices impregnate the bread. Refrigerate for at least 1 hour before serving. Serve lightly chilled.

MOULES AUX PATES A LA NIÇOISE

Mussels with pasta with tomatoes and anchovies — Serves 4–6

Preparation time: 15 minutes + 30 minutes cooking

1 kg (2 lb) mussels

300 ml (½ pint) dry white wine

4 shallots, chopped finely

1 kg (2 lb) tomatoes, skinned, de-seeded and chopped

500 g (1 lb) fresh tagliatelle

50 g (2 oz) can of anchovies, drained and chopped

2 tablespoons capers, drained

1–2 garlic cloves, chopped finely

6 tablespoons chopped fresh herbs such as tarragon, parsley, basil and coriander

35 g (1¼ oz) butter

salt and pepper

Scrub the mussels with a stiff brush and scrape off any barnacles. Let the mussels rest in cold, lightly salted water for 10 minutes. Pull off the beards and discard any mussels that are open.

Using a large pan with a tight-fitting lid, bring the wine to the boil. Add the drained mussels, cover and cook over a high heat, shaking the pan occasionally, for about 5 minutes or until the mussels have just opened. Do not overcook or the mussels will become tough. Discard any which have not opened. Leave to cool and then remove the mussels from their shells. Reserve the mussels and discard the shells. Strain the broth through a muslin-lined sieve into a pan.

Add the shallots to the pan and cook for about 5 minutes. Stir in the tomatoes and cook, uncovered, until soft (about 15 minutes).

Bring a large pot of water to the boil, add some salt and, when the water returns to the boil, add the pasta. Cook the pasta according to the packet instructions.

Meanwhile stir the anchovies and capers into the tomato sauce. Add the mussels and heat just enough to warm through, adding a little more wine if necessary. Add the garlic and herbs at the very last moment. Season with pepper and salt if needed.

Drain the pasta, pour it into a heated serving dish and toss with the butter. Arrange a helping of pasta on individual plates and spoon some of the sauce over the top.

MEAT AND FISH

LE GRAND AIOLI

Preparation time: 1½ hours + 2½ hours cooking + overnight cooling

Serves 10–12

- *1.5–1.75 kg (3½–4 lb) chicken or 1.1 kg (2½ lb) joint of roasting beef*
- *1.1 kg (2½ lb) thick fish fillets e.g. cod, haddock or smoked haddock*
- *1 cauliflower, cut into florets*
- *6 tomatoes, quartered*
- *1 head of celery, cut into sticks*
- *4 heads of chicory, cut in strips lengthways*
- *5 hard-boiled eggs, halved*
- *4 fennel bulbs, trimmed and halved*
- *750 g (1½ lb) small carrots, peeled*
- *500 g (1 lb) fine green beans*
- *1 kg (2 lb) courgettes or asparagus*
- *1 kg (2 lb) new potatoes, scrubbed*

To garnish:

- *a handful of parsley, chopped finely*
- *a bunch of watercress*
- *2 lemons, sliced*
- *2 quantities of aïoli (page 18)*

Aïoli – a garlic mayonnaise – is the centrepiece for this dish and it is indeed a grand affair with the wide variety of vegetables, fish and meat that accompany it. Traditionally aïoli is served with dried salt cod on Fridays, which were once Catholic fast days and are still observed by some. Le Grand Aïoli is served during the summer months to celebrate each village's patron saint. Long tables are set out in village squares and all the local inhabitants gather to enjoy the wonderful spread of food with its pungent sauce. The spread should include both raw and cooked vegetables, as well as hard-boiled eggs, fish, meat or chicken. The choice is vast and should depend on the freshest ingredients available. The list below is just a guide.

The day before you plan on serving Le Grand Aïoli, roast the beef or chicken and allow to cool overnight.

Several hours ahead, preheat the oven to Gas Mark 2/150°C/300°F. Oil a piece of foil large enough to contain the fish. Season the fish with salt (unless it is smoked) and pepper and seal it in the foil. Put the parcel on a baking sheet and bake for 20 minutes or until cooked. Remove from the oven but let the fish cool in the parcel.

Arrange the cauliflower, tomatoes, celery and chicory on another serving dish. Place the eggs on a dish. Steam or boil the fennel, carrots, beans, courgettes or asparagus and potatoes. A multi-tiered steamer is ideal for this; otherwise, use a large quantity of boiling salted water and do the vegetables in batches, scooping them out with a slotted spoon when

Le Grand Aïoli

they are just tender. The vegetables should be just lukewarm when they are served but this is not vital. Place the cooked vegetables on another platter. Cut the chicken into serving pieces or slice the roast beef and arrange on a dish. Sprinkle parsley over the cooked vegetables and garnish the other dishes with watercress and lemon slices. Pass a big bowl of aïoli separately.

DAUBE DE BOEUF

Provençal beef stew — Serves 6

Preparation time: 30 minutes + 24 hours marinating + 4 hours cooking

1.25 kg (3 lb) chuck steak, cut into 5 cm (2-inch) cubes
2 large onions, sliced
2 carrots, sliced
2 celery sticks, sliced
2 garlic cloves, chopped
1 bouquet garni
½ bottle red wine
4 tablespoons olive oil
175 g (6 oz) unsmoked streaky bacon, cut into 5 mm (¼-inch) slices
a small strip of orange zest
300 g (10 oz) tomatoes, skinned and quartered
150 ml (¼ pint) beef stock
salt and pepper
12 Calamata olives or black olives, stoned, to serve.

A special pot-bellied casserole dish called a 'daubière' gives its name to this Provençal stew. The meat is marinated overnight in red wine and olive oil, which both add flavour and help to tenderise the meat. Serve with buttered noodles and a green salad.

Place the meat in a large bowl and add the onions, carrots, celery, garlic, bouquet garni, wine, olive oil and some salt and pepper. Mix together and leave to marinate in the refrigerator for 24 hours.

The next day, preheat the oven to Gas Mark 2/150°C/300°F. Cut the bacon into strips and lay them in the bottom of a heavy, flameproof casserole. Place the marinade vegetables on top of the bacon, lay the meat over this and tuck in the bouquet garni and orange zest. Add the tomatoes. Pour over the marinade and add the stock. Bring slowly to the boil on top of the stove. Cut a piece of baking parchment to fit snugly over the ingredients and then cover with the lid. Put the casserole in the oven and cook gently for 4 hours.

Discard the bouquet garni. Skim off as much surface fat as possible, and check the seasoning. Add the olives to the stew and serve.

BOEUF BRAISE AUX OLIVES NOIRES

Braised beef with black olives — Serves 6

Preparation time: 40 minutes + 3 hours cooking

- *3 tablespoons olive oil*
- *1 carrot, chopped*
- *1 large onion, sliced*
- *2 unsmoked bacon rashers, chopped*
- *1 celery stick, chopped*
- *2 garlic cloves, chopped*
- *1.1 kg (2½ lb) rolled topside of beef*
- *3 tablespoons brandy*
- *250 g (8 oz) tomatoes, skinned and chopped*
- *1 bouquet garni containing 3 sprigs of parsley with stalks, 1 bay leaf, 3 sprigs of thyme and a strip of orange zest*
- *150 ml (¼ pint) beef stock*
- *300 ml (½ pint) red wine*
- *18 small black olives, stoned*
- *2 teaspoons arrowroot*
- *salt and pepper*

The best cuts for braised beef are rump end, rolled topside or chuck steak. Look for meat that is well hung and not too lean, as marbling in the meat will baste the meat as it braises and keep it succulent.

Preheat the oven to Gas Mark 2/150°C/300°F. Heat 2 tablespoons of the oil in a flameproof casserole just large enough to hold the meat, bacon and braising vegetables. Add the carrot and onion and stir for a few minutes to soften. Add the bacon, celery and garlic and cook for several minutes. Transfer the vegetables and bacon with a slotted spoon to a plate. Add the remaining oil to the casserole and brown the meat, turning on all sides.

Warm the brandy in a soup ladle, set it alight and pour it over the beef. When the flames have died down, place the vegetables and bacon back in the pan and add the tomatoes and bouquet garni. Season with salt and pepper. Add the stock and wine, and bring to a simmer on top of the stove. Cut a piece of baking parchment slightly larger than the casserole and cover the meat, tucking it around the edges. Cover the casserole with a tight-fitting lid and place the casserole in the oven. Cook for 2½–3 hours until the meat is tender. Add the olives for the last half hour of the cooking time. Lift the meat from the casserole, and place on a warmed serving platter. Skim the fat from the cooking liquid. This is easily done by floating a piece of kitchen paper over the surface and removing it. Dissolve the arrowroot in a few tablespoons of cold water. Stir in the arrowroot and simmer the casserole on top of the stove to thicken the sauce. Adjust the seasoning, spoon the sauce and vegetables over the meat and serve.

Foie de Veau Moissonière
(Calves' liver moissonière)

Épaule d'Agneau aux Haricots (Shoulder of lamb with haricot beans)

Filet de Bœuf Provençale (Beef fillet stuffed with anchovy butter)

FILET DE BOEUF PROVENÇALE

Beef fillet stuffed with anchovy butter — Serves 6–8

Preparation time: 25 minutes + 30–40 minutes cooking

1.25 kg (3 lb) piece of thick fillet steak, trimmed and tied

3 tablespoons olive oil

For the anchovy butter:

125 g (4 oz) unsalted butter

6 canned anchovies, drained

1 teaspoon lemon juice

2 tablespoons finely chopped fresh parsley

salt and pepper

very finely chopped fresh parsley, to garnish

This is an excellent recipe for entertaining because the preparation can be done well in advance. The beef is briefly roasted ahead of time, then sliced and stuffed with anchovy butter. It has a final roasting while you are eating the first course.

Preheat the oven to Gas Mark 8/230°C/450°F. Season the meat with salt and pepper. Heat the oil in a roasting tin, on top of the stove, and brown the meat on all sides. Roast the fillet in the hot oven for 10 minutes. Remove from the oven and place on a rack to cool completely.

To make the anchovy butter, purée the butter and anchovies in a blender or food processor. Scrape out into a bowl and add the lemon juice, parsley and some pepper. Roll into a sausage shape, wrap in clingfilm and refrigerate.

Preheat the oven to Gas Mark 7/220°C/425°F.

Lay the meat on a piece of foil large enough to enclose it. Remove the string and slice the meat into 5 mm (¼-inch) slices, cutting almost through the meat but leaving just enough to hold the slices together. Cut the anchovy butter into slices and place between each slice of meat. Wrap the meat in foil and roast on a baking sheet in the preheated oven for 20 minutes. This will give you rare slices. If you prefer your meat well done, add another 10 minutes to the roasting time.

To serve, take the meat out of the foil, taking care not to lose the buttery juices. Arrange on a heated platter and scatter with the parsley.

If you are preparing the meat ahead of time, refrigerate it after stuffing it with the anchovy butter slices. Allow enough time for it to come to room temperature before the final roasting.

FOIE DE VEAU MOISSONIERE

Calves' liver moissonière — Serves 4

Preparation time: 10 minutes + 30 minutes cooking

- *500 g (1 lb) calves' or lamb's liver, sliced thickly*
- *1 tablespoon plain flour*
- *25 g (1 oz) butter*
- *4 tablespoons olive oil*
- *500 g (1 lb) mild onions, sliced*
- *1 bouquet garni*
- *175 ml (6 fl oz) red wine*
- *2 tablespoons tomato purée*
- *a pinch of sugar*
- *salt and pepper*
- *2 tablespoons finely chopped parsley, to garnish*

Liver and onions are a well known combination but the French with their culinary expertise manage to scale new heights with these simple ingredients. Keep the liver lightly cooked so that it will stay meltingly tender.

Dry and trim the liver if necessary and dust it with flour. Heat the butter with 1 tablespoon of the oil in a large, heavy frying-pan and fry the liver over a moderate heat for 2 minutes each side. Transfer to a platter and cover loosely with foil.

Add the remaining oil to the pan and stir in the onions. Add the bouquet garni. Cover and cook gently for 15 minutes until the onions are soft. Uncover, raise the heat and stir the onions until they begin to brown. Add the wine, tomato purée and sugar, and cook for another 5 minutes. Taste for seasoning.

Cut the liver into strips and add them to the simmering onions. Allow the liver to heat through but do not cook it further or it will toughen. Discard the bouquet garni and serve immediately, garnished with parsley.

EPAULE D'AGNEAU AUX HARICOTS

Shoulder of lamb with haricot beans — Serves 6

Preparation time: 15 minutes + 8 hours soaking + 1¾ hours cooking

For the beans:

- *375 g (12 oz) dried haricot beans*
- *1 bay leaf*
- *1 onion, stuck with a clove*

Lamb with haricot beans is a favourite French combination and indeed it is a perfect marriage of flavours. Although this is a rustic-looking stew, it is delicious enough for a banquet. The dish reheats perfectly, so it can be prepared one or two days in advance if kept refrigerated.

salt and pepper

For the lamb:

6 large lamb shoulder chops

2 tablespoons oil

1 onion, chopped

3 garlic cloves, chopped

397 g (14 oz) can of chopped tomatoes

a pinch of dried thyme

2 tablespoons flour

a pinch of sugar

salt and pepper

finely chopped parsley, to garnish

Soak the beans for at least 8 hours or overnight in cold water to cover.

Drain the beans, place them in a pan, cover with water and add the bay leaf and onion (but no salt). Bring to the boil and boil rapidly for at least 10 minutes, then simmer until the beans are tender, about 1 hour. Discard the bay leaf and onion. Drain and season with salt and pepper.

Meanwhile trim off any fat from the lamb. Heat the oil in a large frying-pan and brown the lamb on both sides. Season with salt and pepper, and place the lamb in a flameproof casserole. Fry the onion and garlic for a few minutes. Add the tomatoes and thyme, raise the heat and cook for another 8 minutes until the tomatoes have thickened slightly.

Preheat the oven to Gas Mark 3/160°C/325°F.

Heat the casserole on top of the stove, until the juices are bubbling. Sift the flour over the meat, add the sugar and stir the meat so that the flour cooks evenly and begins to brown. Add the tomato mixture, cover, and place in the oven. Cook for 1 hour or until the meat is tender. Spoon off any fat from the surface. Add the beans to the casserole and cook in the oven for another 20 minutes to heat through. Taste for seasoning. Serve garnished with parsley.

SAUCISSES ET POMMES A L'HUILE

Sausages with vinaigrette potatoes — Serves 6

Preparation time: 15 minutes + 20 minutes cooking

1 kg (2 lb) small potatoes

1 kg (2 lb) good-quality pork sausages

3 tablespoons cider vinegar or wine vinegar

2 shallots, chopped very finely

A good olive oil dressing poured over steaming-hot boiled potatoes is absolutely delicious. Try it next time you are serving sausages – it is a great combination.

Cook the potatoes in gently boiling water until tender. At the same time, cook the sausages.

Meanwhile make the vinaigrette. Place the vinegar and shallots in a bowl with salt and

175 ml (6 fl oz) extra-virgin olive oil

3–4 tablespoons finely chopped parsley

salt and pepper

pepper and whisk in the oil. When the potatoes are cooked, drain, place them in a warm bowl, and break them up slightly with a fork. Toss with the vinaigrette and sprinkle with the parsley.

Serve the sausages with the hot potatoes.

PIGEONNEAUX AUX LENTILLES

Pigeon with lentils — Serves 4

Preparation time: 30 minutes + 2 hours cooking

4 wood pigeons

4 tablespoons oil

1 carrot, sliced

1 celery stick chopped

1 onion, sliced

4 tablespoons dry white wine

1 bouquet garni

175 g (6 oz) brown or green lentils

1–2 tablespoons wine vinegar

5 tablespoons extra-virgin olive oil

4 tablespoons finely chopped coriander leaves

1½ teaspoons crushed black peppercorns

salt and pepper

Wood pigeons are available all the year round. They are considered best during the months of May to October because many will be young and plump from the summer crops. A squab is a young pigeon under the age of four months, which is just the right time to eat them. As it is very difficult to tell the age of the pigeon you are buying, I find it best to serve the breasts, which are delicious, and use the often tougher joints to make a stock.

Carefully cut off the breasts from the pigeons by sliding a sharp thin knife down either side of the breastbone (Fig. 1), and remove the skin. Slightly flatten the breasts between two pieces of clingfilm (Fig. 2). Keep refrigerated until needed.

Chop up the rest of the pigeon carcases. Heat 2 tablespoons of the oil in a heavy frying-pan and brown the bones and vegetables. This will take about 10 minutes. Transfer the bones and vegetables to a large pan. Add the wine and boil hard to evaporate some of it, then turn the contents of the frying-pan into the large pan. Add the bouquet garni and enough cold water to just cover the ingredients. Bring slowly to the boil, skim if necessary and simmer, partially covered, for 1½ hours. Strain the stock and degrease it by floating pieces of kitchen paper over the surface. Season with salt and pepper.

Pick over the lentils, removing any small stones. Rinse the lentils and place in a pan. Pour

1

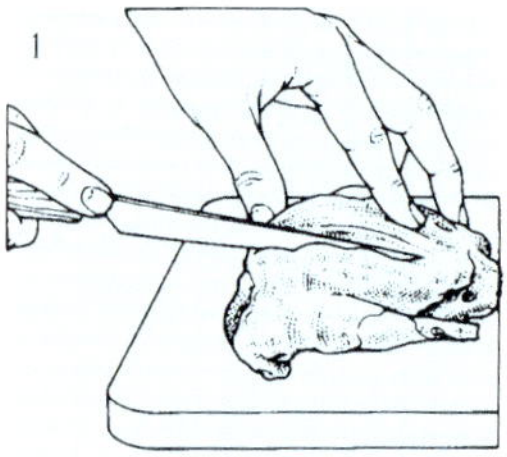

2

over the pigeon stock and simmer, covered, for about 40 minutes. The cooking time for lentils can vary, so check after 30 minutes – they should be tender but should still hold their shape. Drain the lentils and save the stock for soup. Pour the vinegar into a small bowl with some salt. Slowly whisk in the oil to make a vinaigrette and carefully fold it into the lentils. Taste for seasoning. Keep refrigerated if not using immediately. Before serving, reheat in a moderate oven or microwave and scatter the coriander over the top.

Season the breasts on both sides with salt and the crushed black peppercorns. Heat the remaining 2 tablespoons of oil in a frying-pan and, when it is very hot, sear the breasts for 1 minute each side. Reduce the heat to medium and cook for a further 2–3 minutes each side. Press the meat down with a spatula to help keep them flat. Remove them from the pan and let them rest for 5 minutes before slicing and serving on a bed of lentils.

CAILLES AUX RAISINS

Quail with grapes — Serves 4

Preparation time: 30 minutes + 30 minutes cooking

1 shallot, chopped finely

15 g (½ oz) butter

2 tablespoons olive oil

4 chicken livers, thawed if frozen

3 tablespoons cognac

32 white grapes, Italia if possible, peeled and de-seeded

1 teaspoon chopped fresh sage

8 quails

Vine leaves help to keep the quails moist and gently scent the meat. Not surprisingly, the flavour goes particularly well with grapes.

Preheat the oven to Gas Mark 6/200°C/400°F.

Gently fry the shallot in butter and 1 table-spoon of the oil, stirring, until the shallot softens. Add the livers and fry for a few minutes until lightly cooked – still pink on the inside. Transfer to a bowl. Add 1 tablespoon of the cognac to the pan and scrape up any brown bits from the bottom of the pan. Pour this over the livers and add several grapes and the sage. Chop the mixture coarsely and season. Dry the quails with kitchen paper and stuff the cavities

8 vine leaves, fresh or packed in brine

4 unsmoked streaky bacon rashers

175 ml (6 fl oz) game or chicken stock

2 teaspoons arrowroot

salt and pepper

with the liver mixture.

Pour boiling water over the vine leaves to soften and remove any brine, then wipe them dry. Wrap a leaf around each bird and cover with half a rasher of bacon. Hold in place with a piece of string. Place the remaining oil in a roasting tin large enough to hold the quails in one layer. Arrange the quails in the tin and roast for 30 minutes or until cooked. Transfer the quails to a heated platter; remove the string, bacon and vine leaves and discard. Keep the quails warm while you make the sauce.

Discard the fat from the tin, add the remaining cognac and stock and stir to dissolve the tin juices. Strain into a pan. Put the arrowroot in a cup and stir in a few tablespoons of the sauce to dissolve the arrowroot, then add to the sauce in the pan. Add the grapes and heat just long enough to thicken the sauce slightly. Taste for seasoning. Serve the birds with a few tablespoons of sauce and several grapes.

LES SARDINES GRILLEES

Grilled sardines — Serves 4

Preparation time: 15 minutes + 8 minutes cooking

12 fresh sardines, gutted and gills removed but heads left on

1 garlic clove, chopped finely

1 tablespoon dried fennel seeds

olive oil

juice of ½ lemon

salt and pepper

It is wonderful that fresh sardines are now available in this country because they are surely one of the tastiest of all fish. With their glistening silver skin and succulent flesh, I cannot pass them by when I see them on a fish counter. They need only the simplest of preparations – grilling or frying.

Preheat the grill. Rub the sardines with kitchen paper to remove any loose scales. Sprinkle the inner cavities with garlic and fennel seeds, and brush both sides with olive oil. Salt lightly. Grill them under a hot grill about 5 cm (2 inches) below the heat source for about 3–4 minutes each side. Handle them carefully, using a spatula to keep them intact. Place them on a heated platter and squeeze over the lemon juice. Season with salt and pepper, and serve.

Cailles aux raisins (Quail with grapes)

Poulet Farci au Four (Stuffed roast chicken)

Pigeonneaux aux Lentilles (Pigeon with lentils)

POULET FARCI AU FOUR

Stuffed roast chicken — Serves 8

Preparation time: 45 minutes + 15 minutes standing + 45 minutes cooking

4 poussins, each weighing about 450 g (15 oz)
2 tablespoons olive oil
1 teaspoon freeze-dried fines herbes
For the stuffing:
500 g (1 lb) courgettes
25 g (1 oz) butter, softened
4 shallots, chopped finely
75 g (3 oz) ricotta cheese
4 tablespoons fresh breadcrumbs
25 g (1 oz) freshly grated parmesan cheese
1 egg, beaten
salt and pepper

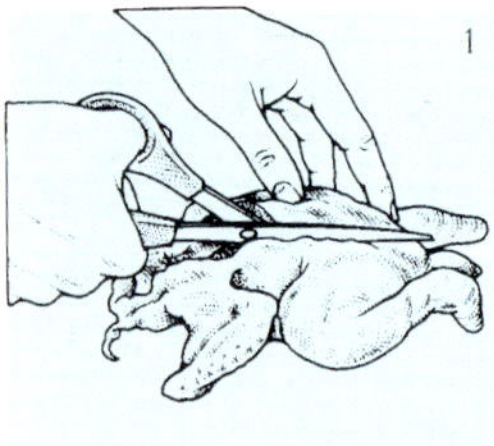
1

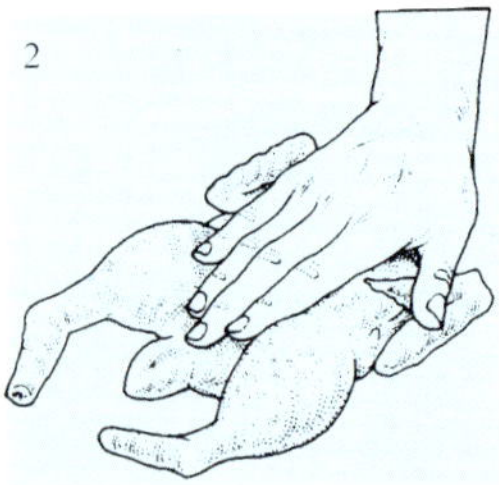
2

This is a delectable way of dealing with poussin and chicken. The stuffing is placed under the skin which keeps the meat beautifully moist and the skin crisp and brown. Poussins are easily cut in half and make just the right portion for a serving. If you prefer to use a chicken, prepare it in the same way but allow 1 hour roasting time.

Place the poussin on its breast. Remove the backbone by cutting down each side with kitchen scissors (Fig. 1). Remove any small bones that may have broken. Turn the bird over, breast up, and flatten the bird with your hand (Fig. 2). Repeat with the other poussins. Rub them with the olive oil and herbs and leave to marinate while you prepare the stuffing.

Grate the courgettes, place them in a colander, sprinkle them with salt and leave for 15 minutes. Take handfuls of the courgettes and squeeze out as much liquid as you can. Melt the butter in a pan and fry the shallots over a very gentle heat until they are soft. Add the courgettes and fry for a few minutes to cook the courgettes slightly and to evaporate any moisture. Cool, then turn into a bowl and mix with the other stuffing ingredients. Season with pepper and salt if necessary.

Preheat the oven to Gas Mark 5/190°C/375°F.

Slip your fingers between the flesh and the skin of the poussin. Spoon in the stuffing and spread it evenly over the legs and breasts. Repeat for each bird.

Bake in an oiled roasting tin for 35–45 minutes, until cooked through. Cover with foil if they brown too quickly. Place on a heated serving platter and serve at once.

MERLANS EN PIPERADE

Whiting with peppers, onions and garlic — Serves 6

Preparation time: 10 minutes + 35 minutes cooking

1 kg (2 lb) whiting or halibut fillets, skinned

1 shallot, chopped finely

125 ml (4 fl oz) dry white wine

125 ml (4 fl oz) fish or chicken stock

2 tablespoons tomato purée

For the piperade:

1 onion, sliced

2 tablespoons olive oil

1 red pepper, de-seeded and sliced finely

1 yellow pepper, de-seeded and sliced finely

1 garlic clove, chopped finely

2 tablespoons finely chopped parsley

salt and pepper

This is an excellent way of serving firm-fleshed fish and is just as delicious cold as hot.

To make the piperade, gently fry the onion in the oil for about 5 minutes, stirring. Add the peppers, garlic, parsley and some salt and pepper. Continue to fry gently, uncovered, until the peppers are almost tender. Adjust seasoning to taste.

Preheat the oven to Gas Mark 4/180°C/350°F. Pat the fish dry with kitchen paper and remove any small bones that you can feel with your fingers. Oil a roasting tin and scatter half the shallot over the bottom. Lay the fish on top and sprinkle the remaining shallot over the fish. Spoon the piperade over the fish and pour the wine and stock around the edge. Lay a cover of baking parchment over the fish. Bring the fish to a simmer on top of the stove before placing it in the oven and baking for 5 minutes. Fish cooks incredibly fast so do not be tempted to leave it in any longer. Tilt the dish and spoon out all the cooking juices into a pan. Add the tomato purée and boil rapidly until you have a thick syrup. Spoon this over the fish and piperade and serve. If serving cold, separate the fish before they cool so that they will not stick together.

Thon Grillé, Sauce Tomate (Fresh tuna steaks with tomatoes)

Merlans en Piperade (Whiting with peppers, onions and garlic)

Brandade de Morue (Purée of salt cod)

BRANDADE DE MORUE

Purée of salt cod | Serves 6

Preparation time: 25 minutes + 24 hours soaking + 15 minutes cooking

750 g (1½ lb) piece of salt cod

300 ml (½ pint) olive oil

1 garlic clove, bruised then chopped finely

284 ml (½ pint) carton of single cream

pepper

finely chopped parsley, to garnish

12 triangles of thin white toast, fried in olive oil, to serve

This is an enormously popular dish in Provence, particularly in the winter months. You will find it in all the charcuteries looking like a giant mound of mashed potatoes, often decorated with black olives. It is the traditional dish served for the fasting supper on Christmas Eve. Salt cod needs to be soaked for at least 24 hours but the preparation is not difficult and the taste is quite addictive. I feel certain this could be a very popular dish in this country with its love for other types of salted and smoked fish.

Soak the salt cod for at least 24 hours, changing the water several times.

Place the cod in a large pan of cold water and bring slowly to the boil. Simmer at the lowest possible heat (the water should just shudder) for 10–15 minutes, until the flesh is just tender. Do not overcook. Drain, remove the bones and skin, and flake with a fork.

Place the cod flakes in a food processor. Heat the oil and garlic in one pan until very hot, and heat the cream until almost boiling in another. Remove the garlic and add it to the cod. With the motor running, add the hot oil and cream alternately to the cod, in a steady slow stream, until they are completely absorbed. You are aiming for a consistency like that of thick creamy mashed potatoes. Season with pepper. Turn out onto a platter and sprinkle the parsley over the top. Arrange the bread triangles around the edge and serve.

Alternatively, the brandade can be made by adding the cod to the pan with the hot oil, then beating hard with a wooden spoon, over a very low heat until the oil is absorbed. Beat in the cream by the tablespoon. Take the cod off the heat if it gets too hot and starts to brown. Continue until the cream is absorbed, then season and turn out on to a platter.

Note: If the brandade is too salty, add 1 or 2 boiled potatoes, mashed, and more cream.

THON GRILLE, SAUCE TOMATE

Fresh tuna steaks with tomatoes — Serves 4

Preparation time: 25 minutes + 10 minutes cooking

- *750 g (1½ lb) fresh tuna steaks, sliced 4 cm (1½ inches) thick*
- *2 tablespoons olive oil*
- *1 tablespoon lemon juice*
- *salt and pepper*

For the tomatoes:

- *6 good-flavoured tomatoes, skinned, de-seeded and chopped*
- *6 tablespoons extra-virgin olive oil*
- *1 garlic clove, finely chopped*
- *several tablespoons of fresh herbs such as chervil, tarragon, chives and parsley, chopped very finely*
- *salt and pepper*

Fresh tuna is becoming more widely available and it is a truly delicious fish, particularly when cut into thick steaks and grilled. It does not have a strong fishy taste despite its dark colour. It tastes more meaty than anything else; if it is not overcooked it will be moist and tender, and there are no bones to worry about.

Rub the fish with pepper and the olive oil, then sprinkle with lemon juice and leave to marinate while you prepare the tomatoes. Combine the tomatoes, olive oil, garlic and half the herbs in a bowl and season with salt and pepper.

Preheat the grill to its highest temperature. Grill the tuna for only about 4 minutes each side, then season with salt. Try to get the outside of the steaks beautifully seared with the inside just cooked through. Place a layer of the uncooked tomatoes on 4 plates and place a portion of the tuna on top. Sprinkle a few herbs over the top and serve.

CABILLAUD AUX HERBES

Cod with a herb crust — Serves 4

Preparation time: 15 minutes + 10 minutes cooking

750 g (1½ lb) cod fillets

75 g (3 oz) fresh breadcrumbs

3 tablespoons mixed fresh herbs including tarragon, thyme and parsley, chopped finely

1 egg, lightly beaten

4 tablespoons olive oil

25 g (1 oz) butter

salt and pepper

lemon wedges, to serve

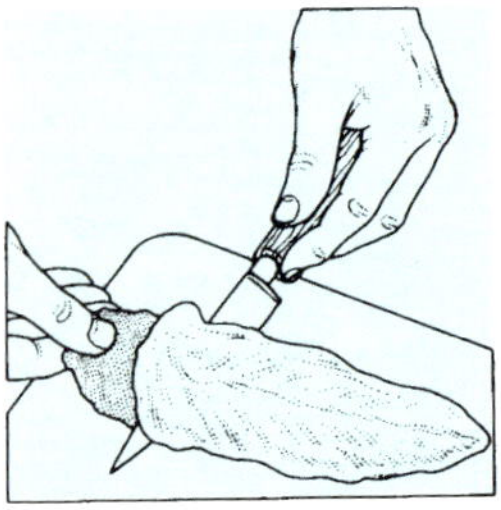

Although cod is not a fish caught in the Mediterranean, it lends itself well to the flavours native to Provence.

To remove the skin from the cod, lay the fish skin-side down on a chopping board. Place a knife with the blade at an angle under the edge of the skin and resting on the board. Pull the skin with the fingers of one hand while you hold the knife firm with the other hand (Fig. 1). The skin will peel away easily. If the fish is very fresh, you can peel off the skin just using your fingers.

Mix the breadcrumbs with the herbs and season with salt and pepper. Season the beaten egg. Moisten the fillets in the egg and then roll them in the herb crumbs. Heat the oil and butter together, add the fish and gently fry on both sides until the fish is cooked and the breadcrumbs nicely browned (about 5 minutes each side depending on the thickness of the fish). Serve with wedges of lemon.

ROUGETS A LA SAUVAGE

Red mullet with herbs — Serves 4

Preparation time: 10 minutes + 15 minutes cooking

4 red mullet, each weighing about 175–200 g (6–7 oz)

100 ml (3½ fl oz) milk

75–125 g (3–4 oz) plain flour, for dusting

125 ml (4 fl oz) extra-virgin olive oil

If necessary, scale and clean the fish without removing the liver. Make slits in each side of the fish 2 cm (¾ inch) apart. Dip the fish into the milk and roll them in the flour, shaking off any excess. Heat the oil in a heavy-bottomed frying-pan, add the fish and cook them for 4–6 minutes on each side. Remove the pan from the

Rougets à la Sauvage (Red mullet with herbs)
Cabillaud aux Herbes (Cod with a herb crust)

1 tablespoon finely chopped fresh thyme

salt and pepper,

1 lemon, cut into slices, to serve

heat, add the thyme to the pan and, with a spoon, baste the fish with the oil and thyme for a few minutes. Remove the fish to a serving platter, and season with salt and pepper. Spoon the thyme with some of the oil over the fish. Arrange the lemon slices around the dish and serve with boiled potatoes.

POULET SAUTE AUX TOMATES

Sauté of chicken with tomatoes, herbs and garlic — Serves 4

Preparation time: 40 minutes + 40 minutes cooking

625 g (1¼ lb) ripe tomatoes, skinned, de-seeded and chopped

4 tablespoons chopped, fresh mixed herbs, such as tarragon, thyme and parsley

1 garlic clove, chopped very finely

1.5 kg (3½ lb) chicken, cut into 8 pieces

2 tablespoons olive oil

1 shallot, chopped very finely

150 ml (¼ pint) dry white wine

150 ml (¼ pint) chicken stock

salt and pepper

Mix together the tomatoes, half the herbs and the garlic. Season with salt and pepper and set aside.

Dry the chicken pieces well with kitchen paper. Heat the oil in a large, heavy pan with a lid. Add the chicken pieces and brown on all sides. Transfer the breasts to a plate. Cover the pan, lower the heat to moderate and cook the legs/thighs for about 6 minutes. Return the breasts to the pan and baste the chicken with the pan juices; season with salt and pepper and the remaining herbs. Cover the pan again and cook for another 15 minutes, turning the pieces once during that time. Prick the chicken with a fork in the thickest part – if the juices run yellow with no trace of pink, it is done. Transfer the chicken to a plate and skim off the fat from the pan. Add the shallot, wine and stock and cook briskly, scraping up any brown bits from the bottom of the pan with a wooden spoon. When the liquid has reduced by half, add the tomato-garlic mixture. When the tomatoes are well heated, return the chicken to the pan and boil for a few minutes more to warm though, basting the chicken with the tomatoes. Serve at once.

SUPPIONS FARCIS

Stuffed squid — Serves 4–6

Preparation time: 1½ hours + 45 minutes cooking

1 kg (2 lb) squid

2 garlic cloves, chopped finely

4–5 tablespoons finely chopped fresh parsley

250 g (8 oz) tomatoes, skinned, de-seeded and chopped

1 green pepper, chopped finely

75 g (3 oz) fresh breadcrumbs

4 tablespoons olive oil

175 ml (6 fl oz) dry white wine

salt and pepper

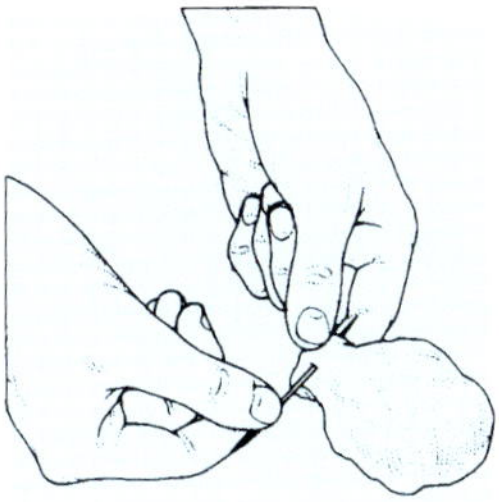

Squid are enjoyed in many Provençal dishes. They blend beautifully with all the flavourful southern vegetables. In this recipe they are stuffed and then simmered in white wine.

To clean the squid, hold the sac in one hand and pull off the head and tentacles with the other. Some of the insides will come away with the head. Cut off the tentacles in front of the eyes. You will feel a tiny hard lump at the top of the tentacles: squeeze it out and discard. Reserve the tentacles. Remove all the rest of the insides of the sac, including the long, flexible quill, and discard. Pour running water into the sac and squeeze out anything remaining inside. Dry with paper towels.

Preheat the oven to Gas Mark 4/180°C/350°F.

Chop the tentacles of the squid and place in a bowl with the garlic, parsley, tomatoes, green pepper and breadcrumbs. Season well with salt and pepper and toss with the olive oil. Stuff the squid loosely with the mixture and close with wooden cocktail sticks (Fig. 1). Do not overstuff the squid or they will split during cooking. Place on an oiled baking sheet or in an ovenproof dish in one layer. Pour over the white wine and bake uncovered for 45 minutes. Remove the sticks, serve with crusty bread.

BAUDROIE A LA PROVENÇALE

Monkfish with garlic, tomatoes and onions — Serves 6

Preparation time: 50 minutes + 25 minutes cooking

- *4 tablespoons olive oil*
- *1 large mild onion, chopped finely*
- *2 garlic cloves, crushed and chopped finely*
- *1.1 kg (2½ lb) monkfish fillets*
- *3 tablespoons plain flour seasoned with salt and pepper*
- *3 tablespoons cognac or brandy*
- *300 ml (½ pint) dry white wine*
- *750 g (1½ lb) ripe tomatoes, skinned, de-seeded and diced*
- *1 tablespoon tomato purée*
- *a big pinch of sugar*
- *2 tablespoons mixed chopped fresh herbs, such as thyme, tarragon and parsley*
- *salt and pepper*

Monkfish is one of the most appreciated fish in France. It has beautiful, firm, sweet-flavoured flesh and is free of bones. This dish is best served with slices of bread brushed with olive oil and grilled.

Heat half of the oil in a heavy-bottomed frying-pan and fry the onion until soft. Add the garlic and cook for a few more minutes. Transfer to a dish and set aside.

Pull off any grey membrane that may be left on the fish and cut the fish into 2.5 cm (1-inch) pieces. Roll them in the seasoned flour. Add the rest of the oil to the pan and lightly brown the fish. Pour 2 tablespoons of the cognac in a soup ladle, warm it over a low heat then set it alight. Pour it onto the fish, stirring, until the flames die out. Transfer the fish to a warm plate and cover lightly with foil.

Return the onions and garlic to the pan. Add the wine, 1 tablespoon of cognac, tomatoes, tomato purée, sugar, herbs and seasoning. Cook over a high heat, stirring occasionally, until the sauce thickens (about 15 minutes). Return the fish to the pan and cook over a very gentle heat for about 5 minutes, or until the fish is just cooked through.

VEGETABLE DISHES

CAROTTES PAYSANNE

Carrots with garlic and parsley — Serves 6

Preparation time: 10 minutes + 30 minutes cooking

4 tablespoons olive oil

1 kg (2 lb) carrots, cut into 1 cm (½-inch) slices

1–2 garlic cloves, chopped finely

200 ml (7 fl oz) water

2 teaspoons sugar

2 tablespoons finely chopped fresh parsley

salt and pepper

Heat the olive oil in a frying-pan with a lid and add the carrots. Sprinkle with salt, and cook gently for 10 minutes, shaking the pan occasionally. Add the garlic, water, sugar and some salt and pepper, and cook for 20 minutes, or until the carrots are tender and have absorbed the water. If any water remains and the carrots are cooked, just boil them hard, uncovered for a few minutes to evaporate the water. Toss with the parsley and serve.

TOMATES A LA PROVENÇALE

Provençal stuffed tomatoes — Serves 6

Preparation time: 25 minutes + 25 minutes cooking

6 medium or 4 large tomatoes

75 g (3 oz) fresh white breadcrumbs

1 garlic clove, bruised then chopped finely

4 tablespoons finely chopped fresh parsley

2 tablespoons shredded fresh basil

5–6 tablespoons extra-virgin olive oil

salt and pepper

These are delicious with all meats and fish.

Cut the tomatoes in half crossways. Gently squeeze out the seeds and juice using your fingers, and discard. Season with salt and leave upside down to drain on kitchen paper.

Preheat the oven to Gas Mark 5/190°C/375°F.

Mix together the breadcrumbs, garlic, parsley, basil, ¼ teaspoon of salt and a few grindings of pepper. Add enough olive oil to moisten the stuffing but still leave it crumbly. Divide the mixture between the tomatoes, mounding it up in the centre. Place in a shallow oiled baking dish. Sprinkle a few drops of olive oil over the top and bake for 20–25 minutes, or until the tomatoes are tender and the filling lightly browned.

PUREE DE POMMES DE TERRE A L'HUILE D'OLIVE

Potato purée with olive oil — Serves 4

Preparation time: 10 minutes + 15 minutes cooking

- *3 large potatoes*
- *150 ml (¼ pint) extra-virgin olive oil*
- *2 sprigs of fresh thyme or 1 teaspoon dried thyme*
- *150 ml (¼ pint) milk*
- *1 garlic clove, bruised then finely chopped*
- *4 shallots, chopped finely*
- *Tabasco sauce*
- *salt and pepper*
- *chopped fresh parsley, to garnish*

Even mashed potatoes become more appetising when they come under a Mediterranean influence.

Boil the potatoes in salted water until cooked. Meanwhile gently heat all but 2 tablespoons of the oil together with the thyme, milk and half of the garlic. When the liquid is hot, remove from the heat. Cool and strain. Fry the shallots and remaining garlic in the rest of the olive oil until soft. Drain the potatoes and mash. Slowly beat enough of the strained liquid into the potatoes to make a smooth purée, then add the shallots. Season well with salt, pepper and a dash of Tabasco. Garnish with chopped parsley and serve.

SALADE D'HARICOTS VERTS A LA CREME

French bean salad with cream — Serves 4–6

Preparation time: 15 minutes + 5 minutes cooking

- *500 g (1 lb) green beans*
- *25 g (1 oz) hazelnuts, sliced*
- *5 tablespoons double cream*
- *1 teaspoon Dijon mustard*
- *2 tablespoons lemon juice*
- *2 tablespoons finely chopped chervil*
- *salt and pepper*

Bring a large pan of water to the boil, add salt and when the water returns to the boil, throw in the beans. Cook, uncovered, until the beans are just cooked (about 4–5 minutes). Drain the beans and plunge them into a large bowl of ice-cold water. Drain again and set aside.

Toast the hazelnuts in a heavy frying-pan, stirring, so that the nuts heat evenly. They should just colour slightly but not brown.

Whisk together the cream, mustard and lemon juice. Season with salt and pepper and add the chervil. Toss the beans in the dressing, and sprinkle with the hazelnuts before serving.

SALADE NIÇOISE

Preparation time: 35 minutes Serves 6–8

750 g (1½ lb) small waxy potatoes, such as Charlotte or Belle de Fontenay

½ small red onion, sliced very finely

175 ml (6 fl oz) extra-virgin olive oil

1 tablespoon cider vinegar

3 tablespoons lemon juice

½ teaspoon Dijon mustard

500 g (1 lb) small green beans

2 different lettuces such as feuille de chêne and Cos

4 good-flavoured tomatoes, skinned and sliced

200 g (7 oz) can of lightmeat tuna in oil, drained

8 hard-boiled eggs, quartered

50 g (2 oz) can of anchovies in olive oil, drained

40 small black olives

4 tablespoons capers, drained

a few tablespoons of fresh mixed herbs such as basil, tarragon, parsley and chervil, chopped finely

salt and pepper

To serve:

olive oil

slices of bread cut from a large baguette

½ garlic clove

salt

This salad, more than anything else, has put Provençal food on the map. Although you may be put off making it by having had inferior versions, it is still, if properly made, one of the great food combinations.

Simmer the potatoes very gently in salted water until just cooked through. Drain and slice them into a bowl when still warm. Add the red onion, 3 tablespoons of the olive oil, the vinegar, a tablespoon of lemon juice and salt and pepper. Toss gently and set aside.

Make a vinaigrette by mixing ½ teaspoon salt, the Dijon mustard and the remaining 2 tablespoons of lemon juice. Slowly whisk in the remaining approximately 125 ml (4 fl oz) of olive oil, drop by drop. Add more lemon juice to taste and season with salt and pepper.

Cook the beans in a large quantity of boiling salted water, uncovered. Drain them after 5 minutes or so, when they are still fairly firm. Refresh them very quickly under cold running water and turn them into a bowl. Toss with a few tablespoons of the vinaigrette.

Arrange the salad leaves in a large shallow bowl. Place the potatoes on the lettuce and then the beans. Add the tomatoes, tuna, eggs, anchovies, olives and capers. Pour over the vinaigrette and toss gently. Sprinkle the herbs over the top.

Preheat the grill. Sprinkle olive oil over the bread and grill on both sides. Lightly rub one side with the cut side of garlic. Sprinkle with salt and serve with the salad.

Salade de Pois Chiches (Chick-pea salad)

Salade de Haricot Verts à la Crème (French bean salad with cream)

Salade Niçoise

SALADE DE POIS CHICHES

Chick-pea salad — Serves 8–10

Preparation time: 30 minutes + 24 hours soaking + 2¼ hours cooking

250 g (8 oz) dried chick-peas

1 bouquet garni

1 tablespoon red wine vinegar

2 tablespoons lemon juice

3 garlic cloves, chopped very finely

3 tablespoons mixed fresh herbs such as tarragon, thyme, chervil and parsley, chopped finely

125 ml (4 fl oz) extra-virgin olive oil

75 g (3 oz) black olives, stoned

1 mild onion, chopped very finely

salt and pepper

Soak the chick-peas for 24 hours in cold water to cover.

Drain the chick-peas and place them in a pan. Cover with fresh cold water and bring to the boil. Boil hard for 10 minutes, reduce the heat, add the bouquet garni and simmer gently for about 2 hours, or until the chick-peas are tender. Check halfway through the cooking time and add more water if necessary.

Mix together the vinegar, lemon juice, garlic, herbs, salt and pepper, then gradually whisk in the oil.

When the chick-peas are tender, drain them and transfer to a serving bowl, discarding the bouquet garni. Toss with the vinaigrette while they are still hot. Mix in the olives and onion and taste for seasoning. Covered and refrigerated, the chick-peas will keep for 4 days.

LES HARICOTS BLANCS EN SALADE

Haricot bean salad — Serves 4–6

Preparation time: 10 minutes + 8 hours soaking + 2 hours cooking

250 g (8 oz) dried haricot beans

125 ml (4 fl oz) extra-virgin olive oil

1 garlic clove, bruised

½ bay leaf

1 sprig of thyme

1 tablespoon tomato purée

Unlike most recipes for dried beans which dress the cooked beans with olive oil and lemon juice, this method simmers the beans in olive oil. The result is the best bean salad ever. The French use demi-sec haricots which need no pre-soaking, will cook in about 45 minutes and are superior in flavour.

Soak the beans for at least 8 hours or overnight in enough cold water to cover.

Heat the oil in a heavy-bottomed pan, add

lemon juice to taste

a few spring onions or 1 small red onion, sliced thinly

salt and pepper

the drained beans, garlic, herbs and tomato purée. Pour in enough water to cover the beans by 2.5 cm (1 inch). Bring to the boil and boil rapidly for at least 10 minutes, then simmer for 1–1½ hours or until the beans are tender, topping up the water if necessary. Remove the lid and boil rapidly until the liquid has reduced to a thick sauce (about 20 minutes). Turn the beans into a serving dish. Remove the herbs and add the lemon juice and the onion slices. Season with salt and pepper and allow to cool before serving.

RAGOUT PROVENÇALE DES QUATRE SAISONS

Seasonal vegetable sauté — Serves 4

Preparation time: 20 minutes + 1 hour cooking

125 ml (4 fl oz) extra-virgin olive oil

5 shallots, sliced

2 garlic cloves, sliced

2 carrots, chopped

2 turnips, chopped

4 small potatoes, scrubbed and diced

2 celery sticks, sliced

2 courgettes, sliced

125 g (4 oz) mushrooms, sliced

250 g (8 oz) broccoli

salt and pepper

To garnish:

12 small black olives, stoned

2 teaspoons chopped fresh chervil or tarragon

This dish can be made at any time of the year with seasonal vegetables. Always use onions or shallots and garlic to give it flavour, but the other vegetables can be changed to whatever is really fresh and catches your eye. Only buy a few of each and try to get an assortment of colour and textures to make the dish more interesting. This is a vegetarian version; however, you could add some diced ham or lightly cooked chicken livers if you are not vegetarian.

Heat the oil in a large heavy-bottomed pan with a lid. Add the shallots, garlic and carrots and cook over a low heat, stirring occasionally, for several minutes. Add the turnips, potatoes and celery, season them with salt and pepper, cover and simmer very slowly until the vegetables are almost tender. Stir the vegetables occasionally and add more oil if necessary. Add the courgettes and mushrooms, cover and cook until they are tender. Meanwhile divide the broccoli into florets and blanch in boiling salted water for 5 minutes. Drain, refresh under cold running water and add to the other vegetables. When all the vegetables are tender, season them and arrange a selection on 4 plates; garnish with the olives and the chervil or tarragon.

TIAN DE LEGUMES

Layered baked vegetables — Serves 6–8

Preparation time: 50 minutes + 1½ hours cooking

- *2 large mild onions, sliced finely*
- *2 aubergines, sliced into rounds 5 mm (¼-inch) thick*
- *8 small courgettes, sliced into rounds 5 mm (¼-inch) thick*
- *12 tomatoes, skinned and sliced 5 mm (¼-inch) thick*
- *3 garlic cloves, chopped finely*
- *3–4 tablespoons chopped fresh parsley or 1–2 tablespoons fresh or dried thyme*
- *150 ml (¼ pint) extra-virgin olive oil*
- *salt and pepper*

This is simple to make because it is just a matter of slicing the vegetables and layering them in a baking dish – the oven does the rest. It improves with keeping, so it can conveniently be made the day before you need it.

Preheat the oven to Gas Mark 4/180°C/350°F. Oil a large 3-litre (5½-pint) gratin dish. Layer the vegetables in the same order as in the list of ingredients, seasoning each layer with garlic, parsley or thyme, salt and pepper and a drizzling of olive oil. Cover tightly with foil and bake for 1¼–1½ hours or until the vegetables are tender. Serve hot or cold.

Tian de Courgettes (Courgette and rice bake)
Tian de Légumes (Layered baked vegetables)

TIAN DE COURGETTES

Courgette and rice bake — Serves 6

Preparation time: 30 minutes + 45 minutes cooking

- *1.25 kg (3 lb) courgettes*
- *75 g (3 oz) long-grain rice*
- *1 large onion, chopped finely*
- *1 tablespoon extra-virgin olive oil*
- *2 garlic cloves, chopped finely*
- *1 tablespoon plain flour*

This tian combines courgettes, cheese and rice and is an excellent accompaniment for grilled fish or chicken – also a useful dish for vegetarians.

Coarsely grate the courgettes into a colander set over a bowl. Mix with 2 teaspoons of salt and leave while you prepare the rice and onions.

Boil the rice in a large quantity of salted water for 5 minutes, then drain and set aside. In a large frying-pan gently fry the onion in the oil for about 8 minutes until translucent. Meanwhile, working over a bowl, take handfuls of the

175–250 ml (6–8 fl oz) milk

1 egg, beaten lightly

65 g (2½ oz) freshly grated parmesan cheese

salt and pepper

courgettes and squeeze the liquid into the bowl. Place the squeezed courgettes in the frying-pan with the onion and add the garlic. Cook, stirring, over a high heat, for 5 minutes then stir in the flour.

Preheat the oven to Gas Mark 5/190°C/375°F. Measure the courgette juices and add enough milk to make 500 ml (18 fl oz). Stir this into the courgette mixture and bring to a simmer, stirring. Remove from the heat, add the rice, the egg and all but 2 tablespoons of the cheese. Season before pouring into a greased 30 cm (12-inch) gratin dish. Sprinkle the remaining cheese over the top and bake for 45 minutes. Serve hot.

GRATIN D'AUBERGINES

Aubergines baked with cheese and tomatoes — Serves 6

Preparation time: 20 minutes + 1 hour standing + 1½ hours cooking

1.25 kg (3 lb) aubergines

4–6 tablespoons olive oil

1 kg (2 lb) ripe tomatoes, skinned, de-seeded and chopped

3 garlic cloves, chopped finely

15–20 fresh basil leaves, shredded

75 g (3 oz) freshly grated Gruyère or parmesan cheese

5 tablespoons fresh breadcrumbs

salt and pepper

Aubergines become bitter if they are not absolutely fresh so always choose very firm, shiny ones and use them straight away. To reduce the amount of fat, you can blanch the slices of aubergine for 2 minutes instead of grilling or frying them in oil. The flavour suffers a little but it is in fact a traditional Provençal way of cooking them and the dish is very tasty either way.

Cut the aubergine into 1 cm (½-inch) slices lengthways. Sprinkle with a little salt and leave in a colander to drain for 1 hour.

Preheat the grill, if using. Blot the aubergine slices dry with kitchen paper. Either brush the slices with olive oil and grill them until lightly coloured, or blanch for 2 minutes in boiling water.

Heat a tablespoon of the oil in a pan and stir in the tomatoes. Cook for a few minutes, then stir in the garlic and half the basil. Season with salt and pepper and remove from the heat.

Preheat the oven to Gas Mark 4/180°C/350°F. Oil an ovenproof gratin dish and place a layer of aubergines in the bottom. Sprinkle with salt and pepper and a little cheese. Layer with some of the tomatoes. Repeat these layers, ending with a good layer of cheese mixed with the breadcrumbs and remaining basil. Bake for about 1 hour. Cover with foil if it browns too quickly.

SALADE MESCLUN

Salad of mixed leaves — Serves 8

Preparation time: 5 minutes

- *75 g (3 oz) rocket leaves*
- *75 g (3 oz) lamb's lettuce*
- *1 feuille de chêne lettuce, small inner leaves only*
- *1 frisée lettuce, small inner leaves only*
- *a small bunch of chervil or tarragon, stems removed*
- *2 cartons of cress*
- *2 teaspoons lemon juice*
- *4–5 tablespoons extra-virgin olive oil*
- *salt and pepper*

In Provence, Salade Mesclun used to be made from an assortment of wild herbs such as rocket, dandelion, lamb's lettuce, purslane and wild chicory. The idea of a mixed green salad consisting of a variety of small leaves – some bitter – is now popular all over France and I suspect it is the influence behind the packages of mixed salad greens available today. In Provence, seed packets of mesclun are sold and a similar, but not as bitter, mixture is sold here. Today many of those original plants and herbs are cultivated and an almost authentic Salade Mesclun can be made. I have given one combination but dozens of others are possible. Aim for a mixture of small leaves – some bitter – and a few fresh herbs.

Place the rocket, lettuces and chervil or tarragon in a salad bowl. Add the cress. In a small bowl, mix some salt with the lemon juice. Whisk in the oil and season with pepper. Pour over the greens and mix with your hands. Arrange a mixture of the leaves on individual plates and serve either after the main course or as a first course.

Variation: Sprinkle some rounds of french bread with olive oil. Toast under the grill. Place a layer of goat's cheese over the bread, dribble some olive oil over the top and grill until the cheese is lightly browned. Serve in the middle of the salad.

LES BROCOLIS EN MARINADE

Marinated broccoli — Serves 4

Preparation time: 5 minutes + 30 minutes cooking

500 g (1 lb) broccoli
2 tablespoons olive oil
75 ml (3 fl oz) dry white wine
juice of ½ lemon
1 bouquet garni
1 garlic clove
1 shallot, chopped finely
2 teaspoons crushed black peppercorns
150 ml (¼ pint) water
salt

Blanch the broccoli for 8–10 minutes in plenty of boiling salted water. Drain, refresh under cold running water and set aside.

Meanwhile place all the other ingredients in a large frying-pan with the water. Bring to the boil and simmer gently, covered, for 15 minutes. Cut the broccoli into small pieces, add to the pan and cook, uncovered, until most of the liquid has evaporated. Taste for seasoning. Serve at room temperature.

FENOUIL BRAISE

Braised fennel — Serves 6

Preparation time: 15 minutes + 1 hour cooking

6 heads of fennel
4 tablespoons olive oil
2 garlic cloves, bruised then peeled
250 g (8 oz) tomatoes, skinned, de-seeded and chopped
salt and pepper

Cut the fennel bulbs in half lengthways. Place the oil and garlic in a heavy-bottomed frying-pan with a lid. Season the fennel and place, cut-side down, in the pan. Cook, covered, over a very gentle heat for 30 minutes, turning occasionally. Add the tomatoes and season with salt and pepper. Cover and cook for a further 30 minutes at the lowest heat possible, until the fennel is tender. If there is too much liquid, boil uncovered for a few minutes until the sauce has almost completely evaporated.

Fenouil Braisé (Braised fennel)
Les Brocolis en Marinade (Marinated broccoli)

BREADS AND DESSERTS

PAIN D'OLIVES

Bread with olive oil and olives — Makes 1 loaf

Preparation time: 40 minutes + rising + 30 minutes cooking

15 g (½ oz) dried yeast (not the easy-blend kind)

2 teaspoons salt

500 g (1 lb) strong white flour

5 tablespoons extra-virgin olive oil

12 Calamata olives, stoned and quartered

Even the small amount of olive oil in this bread moistens and scents it and makes it good enough to eat on its own without butter.

Dissolve the yeast in a scant 300 ml (½ pint) lukewarm water. Mix the salt with the flour, make a well in the centre and add the yeasty water and 4 tablespoons of the olive oil. Knead until the dough is smooth and elastic (5–10 minutes). This can also be done in a food processor. Place the dough in a lightly oiled bowl, cover with a polythene bag and leave to rise in a warm place until more than doubled in size.

Knock the dough down and knead again, this time adding the olives. Shape the dough into a flattish circle about 30 cm (12 inches) in diameter and leave to rise again.

Place a baking sheet in the oven and preheat the oven to Gas Mark 6/200°C/400°F.

Dimple the surface of the dough with your finger and dribble the remaining oil over it. Either slide a floured board under the bread and then quickly slide it off onto the hot baking sheet, or pick it up with your hands and toss it onto the sheet. It does not matter if the shape becomes irregular. Bake for about 30 minutes, or until a deep golden colour. Cool the bread on a wire rack, then wrap it and store in an airtight container. The bread can be reheated in a hot oven for 10 minutes before serving, if desired.

GATEAU AUX PIGNONS

Pine kernel cake — Makes a 20 cm (8-inch) cake

Preparation time: 25 minutes + 40 minutes cooking

50 g (2 oz) pine kernels

175 g (6 oz) self-raising flour

a pinch of salt

125 g (4 oz) butter, at room temperature

125 g (4 oz) caster sugar

finely grated rind of 1 lemon

2 eggs, at room temperature

icing sugar for dusting

This is a lovely, moist cake with a subtle taste provided by the pine kernels.

Preheat the oven to Gas Mark 4/180°C/350°F. Spread the pine kernels on a baking sheet and bake for about 5 minutes to colour very slightly – this will help to bring out their flavour. Grease and line the bottom of a 20 cm (8-inch) cake tin.

Sift the flour and salt onto a square of baking parchment and set aside. Cream the butter, sugar and lemon rind until soft and light. Lightly mix the eggs and beat them into the mixture a little at a time, adding a little of the flour with the last of the eggs. Using a metal spoon, fold in the remaining flour and then the pine kernels. Spoon the mixture into the prepared tin, level the surface and bake for 35 minutes. Partially cool in the tin before turning out onto a wire rack to cool completely. Serve with icing sugar sifted over the top.

TARTE AUX FRUITS

Fruit tart — Serves 8–10

Preparation time: 30 minutes + 55 minutes cooking

150 g (5 oz) caster sugar

125 g (4 oz) unsalted butter

125 g (4 oz) plain flour

1 teaspoon baking powder

a pinch of salt

2 eggs, beaten

This is a wonderful recipe which you can use with all kinds of fruit. A thick cake batter is patted into a tart tin and the fruit is laid over the top. It bakes to a most attractive and delicious cross between a cake and a pie.

Preheat the oven to Gas Mark 4/180°C/350°F.

Cream the sugar with the butter. Sift the flour with the baking powder and salt and stir into the butter mixture, then add the eggs. Mix

500 g (1 lb) peaches

500 g (1 lb) nectarines

juice of ½ lemon

icing sugar for dusting

only enough to blend the ingredients. Spoon the batter into a 23–25 cm (9–10-inch) loose-bottomed flan or cake tin. Smooth the batter into an even layer over the bottom of the tin. Slice the fruit and lay it in circles over the batter. Sprinkle with lemon juice.

Bake for 45 minutes. Sift some icing sugar over the top of the tart, and bake for a further 10 minutes, or until the batter is set and the fruit soft. Serve warm or at room temperature.

TARTE AUX POIRES RENVERSEE

Caramelised upside-down pear tart — Serves 8–10

Preparation time: 35 minutes + 25 minutes cooking

1.75 kg (4 lb) firm but ripe pears such as Rocha, Williams or Packham

175 g (6 oz) sugar

125 g (4 oz) unsalted butter

a pinch of salt

250 g (8 oz) puff pastry, thawed if frozen

crème fraîche, to serve

This is one of the all-time great desserts. The secret for a luscious caramelised pear topping is in cooking the pears on top of the stove before baking the tart in the oven. It is a cousin of the famous apple upside-down Tarte Tatin.

Quarter, peel and core the pears. Toss the pears in a bowl with a few tablespoons of the sugar as you work. Melt the butter and remaining sugar in a 24 cm (9½-inch) ovenproof, cast-iron frying-pan (or you can caramelise the pears in a frying-pan and then transfer them to a cake or flat tin). Arrange the pears in a layer over the butter and sugar. Cook over a high heat, uncovered, for about 20 minutes, until the sugar starts to caramelise and turns a deep golden brown. Carefully swirl the pan around from time to time so that the sugar caramelises evenly. Leave to cool. Transfer to a flat tin if using.

Preheat the oven to Gas Mark 7/220°C/425°F. Roll out a thin circle of pastry slightly larger than the pan you are using. Place the pastry on

Tarte aux Poires Renversée (Caramelised upside-down pear tart)
Tarte aux Fruits (Fruit tart)

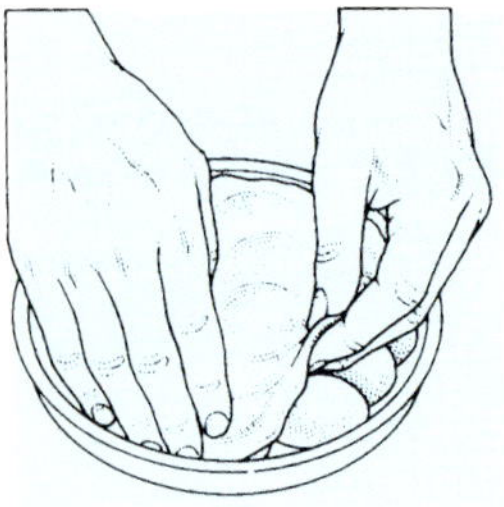

top of the pears, tucking the dough in around the edges (Fig. 1). Bake for 10 minutes or until the pastry is golden brown. Lower the oven to Gas Mark 4/180°C/350°F and bake for another 10–15 minutes. Remove the tart from the oven and cool slightly. Using oven gloves, place a large heatproof serving plate on top of the tart. Invert the pan smartly so that the tart falls onto the serving dish. If any pears stick to the bottom of the pan, remove them with a spatula and replace on the tart. Serve warm with the crème fraîche passed separately. The tart can be successfully reheated in a moderate oven for about 15 minutes.

POIRES ET PRUNEAUX AU VIN ROUGE

Pears and prunes cooked in red wine — Serves 8

Preparation time: 20 minutes + 1 hour soaking + 40 minutes cooking

- *24 dried prunes*
- *150 g (5 oz) sultanas*
- *8 firm but ripe or nearly ripe pears*
- *1 bottle red wine, such as a Côte du Rhône*
- *375 g (12 oz) sugar*
- *3 strips of orange zest*
- *juice of 1 lemon*
- *2 bay leaves*
- *2 cloves*
- *1 cinnamon stick*
- *a few blades of mace*
- *½ teaspoon coriander seeds*
- *½ teaspoon allspice berries*
- *4 large oranges*
- *284 ml (½ pint) double cream, to serve*

A lovely dessert for the winter months.

Soak the prunes and sultanas in warm water for 1 hour. Peel the pears but leave the stalks on. Place the wine, sugar, orange zest, lemon juice and spices in a pan. Squeeze the juice from one of the oranges and add it to the pan. Add the pears and poach gently, covered, for 15 minutes. Add the drained prunes and sultanas and continue to cook, uncovered, until the pears and prunes are soft.

Meanwhile peel and cut the remaining oranges into segments. Remove the pan from the heat and add the orange segments to the pan. When the fruit is cool, remove the cinnamon stick and spices, then transfer the fruit with a slotted spoon to a glass serving bowl. Boil the syrup fiercely for a few minutes, to reduce and thicken it, then strain over the fruit. Serve with the cream passed separately.

GATEAU MOUSSE AU CHOCOLAT

Chocolate mousse cake — Serves 10–12

Preparation time: 35 minutes + 1 hour chilling

- *200 g (7 oz) plain deluxe cooking chocolate*
- *125 g (4 oz) continental deluxe cooking chocolate*
- *568 ml (1 pint) carton of double cream, at room temperature*
- *2 tablespoons milk*
- *2 tablespoons cognac or brandy*
- *unsalted butter for greasing*
- *unsweetened cocoa powder, sifted*
- *crème fraîche, to serve*

More a mousse than a cake, this is one of those desserts that make chocolate lovers gasp with pleasure after the first melting mouthful. It takes no time to make but does need to be assembled with care.

Lightly grease a 24–25 cm (9½–10-inch) cake tin with unsalted butter and line the bottom with baking parchment.

Break the chocolate into small pieces and place in the top of a double pan set over hot water. Cover and leave until the chocolate has melted. Stir the chocolate and let it stand until it has just cooled to blood temperature.

The cream should be cool, but not cold. (If necessary place the container of cream in a bowl of hot water for a few minutes.) Whisk the cream with the milk and cognac until it reaches the ribbon stage – when the whisk is lifted you can make a ribbon trail that will keep its shape. Do not over-whip. Fold the chocolate into the cream using a large metal spoon. Turn into the tin and smooth the top with a palette knife. Cover the tin with clingfilm and refrigerate for at least 1 hour or overnight.

Before serving, slip a knife around the edge of the tin. Set the bottom of the tin in hot water for 10 seconds. This will just begin to melt the cake so that it will turn out with ease. Turn out onto a serving plate. Remove the baking parchment disc, and smooth the top with a palette knife before sifting a fine covering of cocoa powder over the top of the cake. The cake should be left at room temperature for 1–2 hours before serving. Serve with a bowl of crème fraîche passed separately.

If you have a suitably sized spring-form cake tin, this dessert is even easier as it then needs no turning out.

Croissants de Provence (Almond crescents from Provence)

Gâteau Mousse au Chocolat (Chocolate mousse cake)

Poires et Pruneaux au Vin Rouge (Pears and prunes cooked in red wine)

CROISSANTS DE PROVENCE

Almond crescents from Provence — Makes about 24

Preparation time: 45 minutes + 20 minutes cooking

175 g (6 oz) ground almonds

150 g (5 oz) caster sugar

1 tablespoon apricot jam, sieved

½ teaspoon vanilla essence

2 large egg whites, lightly beaten

75 g (3 oz) chopped almonds

1 tablespoon icing sugar

3 tablespoons milk

butter for greasing

flour for rolling

If you like macaroons you will enjoy these pretty biscuits.

Mix the ground almonds with the caster sugar in a bowl. Add the jam and vanilla essence. Gradually stir in about two-thirds of the egg white – just enough to form a thick dough which can be worked by hand.

Preheat the oven to Gas Mark 4/180°C/350°F. Grease 2 baking sheets with butter. Divide the dough into pieces the size of walnuts and roll out on a floured surface to form cylinders about 8 cm (3 inches) long. Paint the surfaces of each stick with the remaining egg white and roll in the almonds. Place the cylinders on the baking sheets, bending at the ends to form crescents. Bake for 20 minutes at the given temperature then turn off the oven and leave the crescents in the oven for another 20 minutes.

Dissolve the icing sugar in the milk. When the crescents are cooked, take them out of the oven and paint them with the milk to give them a shiny glaze. Leave to cool on a wire rack. Store in an airtight container until required.

TORTE DE BLETTES

Apple, swiss chard and pine kernel pie — Serves 8

Preparation time: 35 minutes + 50 minutes cooking

For the pastry:

425 g (14 oz) plain flour

a pinch of salt

25 g (1 oz) icing sugar

250 g (8 oz) butter, or half butter and half margarine

1 egg yolk

3–5 tablespoons iced water

For the filling:

2 tablespoons rum

75 g (3 oz) raisins

500 g (1 lb) fresh swiss chard or spinach leaves

500 g (1 lb) dessert apples such as Cox's

65 g (2½ oz) pine kernels

65 g (2½ oz) brown sugar

75 g (3 oz) mild Cheddar, grated

2 tablespoons redcurrant jelly

2 eggs

grated zest of 1 lemon

salt

This is a traditional and much-loved dessert from Nice. The surprising combination of apples with swiss chard (or spinach) and cheese is most successful. If you reduce the sugar, you can serve this as a savoury course.

To make the pastry, sift the flour, salt and sugar together into a bowl. Cut the butter into small pieces and rub into the flour until the mixture resembles coarse breadcrumbs. Using a fork, mix in the egg and just enough water to bind the dough together. Shape the dough into 2 discs, one larger than the other. Wrap in clingfilm and refrigerate while you prepare the filling.

Place a baking sheet in the centre of the oven and preheat to Gas Mark 5/190°C/375°F. Heat the rum and raisins together, remove from the heat and leave to infuse. Wash the swiss chard or spinach and place in a pan with the water still clinging to the leaves. Add a sprinkling of salt and cook, stirring, just long enough for the leaves to wilt. Drain well, squeezing out any excess liquid. When cool, chop the swiss chard or spinach and place in a bowl. Quarter, core, peel and slice the apples and add to the bowl. Toast the pine kernels in a dry frying-pan for a few minutes, to colour slightly. Add them to the bowl along with the sugar, cheese, redcurrant jelly and lemon zest. Lightly whisk the eggs and add to the mixture. Add the raisins and rum. Mix all the ingredients together well.

Roll out the larger disc of dough and line a 25 cm (10-inch), 5 cm (2-inch) deep tart tin. Spoon the filling into the pie shell. Roll out the smaller disc as thin as possible and cut a circle slightly bigger than the diameter of the tin. Place on top of the filling. Cut off any excess pastry. Seal the edges with a fork. Make a few slits in the top of the pie and bake on the hot baking sheet for 45–50 minutes. Serve warm or at room temperature.

TARTE AU CITRON

Lemon tart — Serves 6–8

Preparation time: 45 minutes + 20 minutes chilling + 1 hour cooking

For the pastry:
200 g (7 oz) plain flour
½ teaspoon salt
100 g (3½ oz) unsalted butter, diced
1 egg yolk
3–4 tablespoons cold water
For the filling:
2 eggs
125 g (4 oz) sugar
grated zest and juice of 2 lemons
125 g (4 oz) melted butter
50 g (2 oz) ground almonds

Lemon tarts are made all over France but only in Provence do they add ground almonds to the lemon filling. The flavours combine to create a succulent and most delicious treat. Use unwaxed lemons, but if you cannot find any, just scrub ordinary lemons in warm water to remove the wax.

To make the pastry, sift the flour and salt together into a bowl. Using your fingers, rub the butter into the flour until it resembles coarse breadcrumbs. Stir with a fork, adding the egg yolk and just enough water to bind the mixture together. Form the dough into a disc, cover in clingfilm and refrigerate for 20 minutes.

Place a baking sheet in the centre of the oven and preheat to Gas Mark 6/200°C/400°F.

Roll out the dough and line a deep 25 cm (10-inch) pie tin. Line the pastry with a piece of crumpled baking parchment, pressing it well into the corners. Fill with uncooked dried beans. Bake for 12 minutes or until the pastry is set and golden. Remove the paper and beans and bake for a further 5–6 minutes. Remove from the oven and leave to cool slightly. Reduce the oven temperature to Gas Mark 4/180°C/350°F.

Meanwhile make the filling: beat the eggs with the sugar over a bowl of hot water until the mixture is thick enough to leave a ribbon trail when the whisk is lifted. Stir in the zest and lemon juice, then add the butter and ground almonds. Set the pie crust on the hot baking sheet and pour the mixture into the shell. Bake for 40 minutes or until the filling is golden brown and set, covering the edges of the pastry with foil part-way through if they brown too much. Serve at room temperature.

Tarte au Citron (Lemon tart)
Figues au Gratin (Grilled figs)

FIGUES AU GRATIN

Grilled figs — Serves 6–8

Preparation time: 15 minutes

- *16 ripe fresh figs*
- *about 3–4 tablespoons clear honey*
- *200 ml (7 fl oz) double cream*
- *2 tablespoons cognac or brandy*
- *2 tablespoons caster sugar*

A very simple and attractive pudding to enjoy when figs are in season. The figs can be prepared several hours in advance, then grilled just before serving.

Preheat the grill. Remove the stalks from the figs. Cut the figs in half vertically and lay them in a large gratin dish, cut-side up. Place a dab of honey on each fig. Whip the cream, add the cognac and sugar and whip a little more to thicken. Place a teaspoon of cream over each fig. Before serving, place the figs quite far below the hot grill, until the cream has turned light brown. This can happen quickly so keep an eye on them. Place the figs on a serving platter and serve while hot.

FIGUES SAINT-JEAN-CAP-FERRAT

Figs with crème fraîche — Serves 6–8

Preparation time: 10 minutes + 30 minutes macerating

- *18 ripe black figs*
- *200 ml (7 fl oz) carton of crème fraîche*
- *2 tablespoons caster sugar*
- *2 tablespoons cognac*

As a young woman I spent my first French holiday at a friend's rented villa in Saint-Jean-Cap-Ferrat. A wonderful but temperamental cook worked in the house and the dishes she prepared were a new and thrilling experience for me. I wish I had paid more attention and discovered some of her secrets, but I do remember this very simple yet delicious dessert. Make this in the autumn when figs are at their best and most readily available; this little pudding can become a seasonal treat.

Cut the figs into quarters. Mix the crème fraîche with the sugar and cognac. Pour over the figs and leave to macerate for at least 30 minutes before serving. It can be made in advance and refrigerated, but serve at room temperature.

INDEX TO RECIPES

Cover design: Moore Lowenhoff
Cover illustration: Kiki Lewis
Text design: Ken Vail Graphic Design
Photography: Laurie Evans
Styling: Lesley Richardson
Food preparation: Janice Murfitt
Illustration: John Woodcock
Typesetting: Goodfellow and Egan